Good Housekeeping

Spills,
Spots
and Stains

First published in the United Kingdom in 2007 by
Collins & Brown
10 Southcombe Street
London, W14 0RA

An imprint of Anova Books Company Ltd

This edition published 2008 for Index Books Ltd

The *Good Housekeeping* website address is www.goodhousekeeping.co.uk

ISBN 978-1-84340-394-4

A CIP catalogue for this book is available from the British Library.

10 9 8 7 6 5 4 3 2

Reproduction by Classic Scan, Singapore
Printed and bound by SNP Leefung Printers Limited, China

This book can be ordered direct from the publisher.
Contact the marketing department, but try your bookshop first.

www.anovabooks.com

Good Housekeeping

Spills, Spots and Stains

Helen Harrison

COLLINS & BROWN

Contents

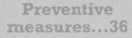

DON'T PANIC!
THE ANSWER TO YOUR STAIN PROBLEM IS HERE

We've all done it – dropped food on a precious garment, found a mark on the carpet, spotted a stain on the furniture – and then panicked. Should you wet it or leave it to dry? Do you have the killer stain remover in your kitchen cupboard – or, better still, about your person while you're out and about? And isn't there some piece of folklore involving vinegar or a hot iron? Or should you just play safe and have it dry cleaned? Armed with this book, you'll have all the answers – secure in the knowledge that every single piece of advice has been tried and tested in the famous Good Housekeeping Institute.

You'll find everything you need here, including precise instructions for removing seventy-five specific stains – from avocado to vomit and from mascara to tar – on fabrics, carpets and other surfaces around the home and in the office. There's also a clear explanation of the different types of stain and how to treat them. Get it wrong and you could make things worse, so do check the Need to Know section. There's little you can do to avoid accidental spills – short of giving up food, drink, visitors and life in general – but prevention is better than cure, so we've also included a section on cleaning and caring for your clothes and other fabrics, surfaces and furnishings.

TRIED, TESTED AND TRUSTED

'Help! I've got lily pollen on my new white jacket. There's mud on the carpet, red wine on the tablecloth, a heat mark on the coffee table, lipstick on his collar…'

Sounds grim? Solving problems like these is all in a day's work for the Good Housekeeping Institute's consumer team. Challenged on a daily basis to find ways to remove everything from beetroot to bicycle grease from places they don't belong, our researchers make it their business to test every cleaning and stain removal remedy they can find.

There's more to it than dabbing a few different products on our own after-dinner disasters, though. First, the staining substance has to be collected or made up in a standard way. Grass, for instance, has to be snipped from a nearby lawn, scrunched into a ball and scrubbed on to the fabric to replicate an outdoor accident. Precisely equal quantities of tea or coffee, of a standard strength, are spooned out. Exactly measured amounts of mud, or peaches and raspberries (we track them down, even out of season), are smeared on to swatches of fabric or carpet. Blood's a tricky one these days, now that butchers no longer sell it – so we use raw steak as a substitute.

Preparing the swatches is a painstaking job in itself. Each one measures 10x10cm, cut from white woollens, cotton, silk or linen material or from pale 80% wool 20% nylon carpet. How many swatches is that? The answer is however many it takes to try out all suitable stain removers, including household remedies as well as proprietary products, on each stain, on each type of fabric or carpet. Oh, and then multiply that number by two – because we need to know not only how effective a method would be if you managed to treat it straight away but also what would happen if you left the spill overnight before trying to remove it. So testing just 10 stains could mean preparing 1,000 swatches, each of which has to be labelled with the type of stain and the removal method to be used.

Now it's time to start trying to get rid of the marks. That means a short pause to check the manufacturer's instructions. Some are liquids you dab on, some are aerosol sprays, others have to be made up into a paste before applying or need to be added immediately before washing. One product may have to be left on for 10 minutes while another may claim to give instant results. With household remedies and old wives' tales, our researchers may have to experiment before finding the quantities and timing that do the trick. One recent method we tried – after a hint from a cricketing colleague – was toothpaste as a way of removing grass stains from cotton. It worked, but only if the toothpaste was plain and free of stripes or blue or red colouring, which can leave a fresh stain of their own.

Most fabric stain removers have their work completed by laundering, so we don't judge their effectiveness until our stained and treated swatches have been through a wash programme – one that matches the type of fabric, of course. Many stains will come out without any extra treatment if they're washed at the highest temperature for that fabric with an appropriate detergent. Sounds simple? Yes, but it's not an experiment you'll want to make with your own precious clothes, which is why we try it out on every single fabric and stain.

When our swatches are washed – and ironed, making it easier to see exactly how clean they are – researchers check in a special light box how well each remedy has worked. Only the ones that work best have made it into this book.

Judith Gubbay
Consumer Director,
Good Housekeeping

Help!

I've got
lily pollen
on my new
white jacket

THE
GOOD HOUSEKEEPING
INSTITUTE

Within two years of its launch in 1922, *Good Housekeeping* magazine set up its own Institute to test products and recipes, provide advice and champion the rights of consumers.

As well as producing test reports and many other practical features in the magazine and on our website at www.goodhousekeeping.co.uk, the Good Housekeeping Institute's consumer team responds to more than 7,000 requests a year for information and advice, many of them about cleaning and stain removal.

1

Need to know

EVERYTHING
YOU NEED TO KNOW
ABOUT STAINS

In this section you will find detailed information on stain-removal methods and techniques, the four basic types of stain, and all the products you'll need to remove them successfully, including remedies that are environmentally friendly.

THE GOLDEN RULES OF STAIN REMOVAL

What makes a stain a stain? This may seem a strange question, but the truth is that the word 'stain' is overused. A true stain occurs only when a chemical reaction takes place between the staining agent and the fibres of a fabric or surface, leaving a **PERMANENT** blemish or mark. Thankfully, this is not the case with most of the spills, splashes and spots we generally think of as stains. In fact, with the correct approach and the right products, many 'stains' can be removed quite easily. You simply need a little knowledge and understanding of how best to go about doing it! Without this information, your chances of success are much lower and you could even make the problem worse. In this section, you will find a simple explanation of the underlying principles of stain removal, as well as our Top Twenty do's and don'ts.

Basic principles

Understanding the four main principles involved in the successful removal of stains will help you to get better results, so here is the scientific bit!

ABSORB IT
The first thing to do is to lift off or soak up as much of the staining substance as possible from the fabric or surface, using absorbents such as talcum powder and paper towels.

DISSOLVE IT
Residue that can't be absorbed needs to be dissolved. However, different substances have differing solubility in solvents. For example, blackcurrant juice is soluble in water, while the curcumin colouring in turmeric requires an alcohol, such as methylated spirits, for it to dissolve. Therefore it's important to consider which solvent will be most effective on a particular stain.

**USE A DETERGENT**
Greasy or fatty stains, such as gravy, will not dissolve in water.

To get rid of the rest of the stain use detergent. Detergents work by changing the surface tension of water so that it can flow more freely into the crevices of a fabric. Molecules in the detergent form a chemical link between the staining particles and the water. When the detergent is rinsed away, the water and stain are taken with it.

USE A CHEMICAL REACTION
If principles 1 to 3 don't work, it's down to chemical reactivity, using agents such as bleach and enzymes. Bleach strips molecules of the electrons that give them colour, therefore making the stain invisible. Enzymes work by breaking down the bonds that hold the amino acids in proteins together. Separated, the amino acids are more soluble in water, so can be more easily rinsed away to remove the stain.

Ten things you should always do to a stain

(1) ACT QUICKLY The golden rule of stain removal. The faster you get to grips with an offending spill, the greater your chance of removing it. If a stain is allowed to dry you run a much greater risk of it becoming permanent, and in a few cases, you may even have to accept that the item cannot be saved.

(2) BLOT THOROUGHLY With a water-based stain, remove as much as possible by blotting with white paper towels or a clean, white, cotton cloth. For very small stains, use cotton buds. Change the blotting material as soon as it becomes soiled. For a greasy stain, sprinkle with cornflour or talcum powder. Leave it to absorb the grease for a few minutes, then remove using a soft brush.

(3) LIFT For more solid stains, gently scrape off lumpy bits with a blunt knife. On powdery dry stains, such as pollen, use sticky tape wrapped around your fingers to lift debris.

(4) WORK FROM THE OUTSIDE INWARDS Always start at the edge of the stain and work towards the centre. That way, you will avoid spreading it and causing further damage.

(5) TREAT FROM THE UNDERSIDE WHERE POSSIBLE The idea is to push the stain out rather than further in. When flushing with water, always run the water through from the 'wrong' side of the stain.

CHECK THE CARE LABEL Don't ruin a favourite item by panicking and throwing it straight into the washing machine, only to realize later that it's 'dry-clean only' and see it emerge from the machine sized to fit a Barbie doll! Read the care label (see Understanding Laundry Symbols, page 55).

 READ THE INSTRUCTIONS This may seem obvious, but when using any stain-removing product, always follow the manufacturer's instructions. They are given for good reasons, so ignore them at your peril.

 TEST FIRST Always test any stain remover on an inconspicuous area first to check for colourfastness or other potential damage.

RINSE BEFORE WASHING If you have used any product to spot-treat a stain, be sure to rinse it out with plenty of cold water before washing the item. This will prevent any undesirable chemical reactions occurring between the product and detergent.

DRY NATURALLY After treating a stain, always allow the garment or fabric to dry naturally. Heat from a tumble-dryer or iron can fix any remaining traces of the stain. If it's been allowed to dry naturally, you may still have a chance to remove the remnants with a second treatment.

…And ten things you should never do

(1) DON'T USE HOT OR EVEN WARM WATER Flushing a fresh stain with hot water may seem like the obvious thing to do, but it can be disastrous. Hot water can permanently set some stains, particularly those with a protein base, such as blood. Always flush with cool water.

(2) DON'T RUB FURIOUSLY Rubbing a stain frantically is likely to make it spread further, and may also damage the weave of the fabric. You'll have more success if you dab it gently.

(3) NEVER OVER-WET WITH STAIN REMOVER Light, repeated applications work much better than flooding a stain. This is particularly important on carpets and upholstery, which are awkward to rinse and get dry. Don't be surprised by the number of times you will need to repeat the process. Perseverance is the key!

(4) NEVER WORK SOAP INTO FRESH STAINS Bar soap, soapflakes and detergents containing soap can set stains, particularly those that include tannin-based pigments, such as coffee, red wine and tea.

(5) NEVER PUT SALT ON A RED WINE STAIN The salt may well absorb the liquid, but as with soap, it will also set tannin pigments permanently. The same principle applies to coffee, tea or cola and any other stain containing tannin.

(6) **NEVER MIX STAIN-REMOVAL PRODUCTS** Unless you're a chemistry boffin, it's a bad idea to mix different products. Chemicals can react together with very unpleasant consequences, particularly chlorine bleach with ammonia, which when combined will create lethal chlorine gas.

(7) **DON'T USE ENZYME-BASED PRODUCTS ON SILK OR WOOL** Both of these are protein fibres, and an enzymic product will have the same 'digesting' effect on them as it does on any protein-based stain – while this may be desirable on blood or eggs, it's less welcome on your favourite cashmere sweater!

(8) **NEVER USE CHLORINE BLEACH ON SILK OR WOOL** These fabrics are too delicate to withstand the harsh effects of bleach. Bleach is also unsuitable for many synthetic fabrics. Check the care label (see Understanding Laundry Symbols, page 55).

(9) **NEVER TRY TO REMOVE STAINS FROM ANTIQUE FABRICS** When baby vomits on your family's precious heirloom christening gown, don't try to remove the stains yourself. Antique fabric is particularly delicate and therefore treatment is best left to the professionals (see Specialist Product Directory, page 183).

(10) **DON'T GIVE UP** Be patient. Some stains respond slowly and you may need to repeat procedures several times before you get results.

Don'ts

WARNING

IMPORTANT PRECAUTIONS

Always observe the following precautions when using hazardous cleaning agents such as chlorine bleach and methylated spirits:

⚠ Read and take notice of ALL warnings on the label.

⚠ Don't breathe in vapours.

⚠ Work in a well-ventilated area.

⚠ Use only a small amount of the cleaning agent at one time, and keep the bottle capped to prevent accidents.

⚠ Don't smoke or work near any open flame.

⚠ Any spillage on the skin should be wiped with a paper towel and rinsed off at once. If you experience a bad reaction, consult a doctor immediately.

⚠ Wear rubber gloves if you have sensitive skin or if you are handling corrosive chemicals.

TYPES OF STAIN AND HOW TO DEAL WITH THEM

Stain removal is an inevitable and troublesome part of caring for fabrics and surfaces. We've all thrown away a treasured item of clothing thinking that the red wine splashed down its front just isn't going to come out in the wash. To help prevent this happening over and over again, it's useful to have an understanding of the different types of stains that exist and how best to treat them. Some stains come out if you simply rinse them in water, but you also need to know whether the water used should be cold or hot. Some stains require a solvent or detergent, while others might need bleaching or digesting by enzymes to get rid of them. This section will help you identify stain types and choose the most suitable line of attack for dealing with each one.

The four main offenders

There are four main types of stain you need to be aware of: grease-based, pigment-based, protein-based and the more complex combination stains. Each requires a slightly different approach for successful removal.

GREASE-BASED STAINS

Grease-based stains are caused by items such as butter, cooking oil, mayonnaise, bacon fat, suntan lotion and face creams. They are not soluble in water and can be tricky to get rid of completely. As always, you'll have the most success if you act quickly.

The rules Gently scrape off any solid or lumpy parts of the stain with a blunt knife, then soak up as much of the grease as you can with white paper towels. Lightly sprinkle the stain with talc or cornflour and allow to stand for a few minutes so that it can absorb the grease, then remove the powder with a soft brush. Any remaining grease must be dissolved, and for that you'll need an alcohol-based solvent such as methylated spirits. Gently dab at the stain with the solvent and allow it to evaporate. Then work a little liquid detergent into the stained area and leave for a few minutes. Machine-wash as normal on as high a temperature as the fabric allows.

PIGMENT- AND TANNIN-BASED STAINS

These stains are caused by coloured products and food. Examples are fruit juice, food colouring, coffee, perfume and grass. The stains are usually water-soluble (unless in combination with other substances), but can be difficult to remove if not treated immediately.

The rules Blot up as much of the stain as possible with white paper towels or a cloth, then flush or sponge with cold water containing a few drops of white vinegar, and blot again. If the stain still looks bad and the fabric allows it, pre-soak in a proprietary oxygen-based, colour-safe bleaching product for as long as is recommended by the manufacturer. Follow up by machine-washing with detergent at as high a temperature as the fabric allows. Dry naturally.

⚠ WARNING

TANNIN

Certain types of pigment-based stains also contain tannin (eg red wine, tea, perfume, beer). For these stains, there is one very important rule to remember, and that is to never use salt (or, for that matter, ordinary bar soap). Both of these products can set a tannin stain permanently. So please, please, don't resort to that old wives' tale that suggests sprinkling salt on a red wine stain — it simply won't work!

PROTEIN-BASED STAINS

Egg, vomit, blood and faeces are examples of protein-based stains. Although protein is quite straightforward to remove, it can coagulate and set into textile fibres at even relatively low temperatures, so the key thing is never to use very hot water.

The rules Lift off as much of the stain as possible, using a blunt knife and white paper towels. Soak the item in cold water. Adding a biological pre-soaking agent (see Tools for the Job, pages 26–31), such as Biotex, will also help. This type of product contains enzymes that 'digest' proteins and break them down. Be careful though – certain fabrics, such as silk and wool, are themselves protein fibres and can be damaged by products containing enzymes. Always check the manufacturer's instructions. After soaking, machine-wash at a temperature below 30°C.

COMBINATION STAINS

As the name suggests, these are stains that have more than one component. Good examples are gravy (protein and grease), ice cream (protein, grease and pigment), candle wax (pigment and grease), lipstick (pigment and grease) and crayon (pigment and grease). Unsurprisingly, they are complex to remove and you will have to adopt a two-step approach to deal with them.

The rules Treat the greasy or protein part of the stain first, following the rules given previously, right up to before the machine-washing process, then wash at as high a temperature as the fabric allows. Next, follow the instructions for treating pigment-based stains.

MYSTERY STAINS

When a mysterious murky splodge appears on one of your favourite items, how do you go about identifying and removing it? Smell, location and colour may give you a clue. Food and drink typically appear on the front of garments, while the smudge on the collar of a man's shirt may be lipstick! As a rule of thumb, begin with the stain-removal method least likely to cause damage. If the item is washable, start by soaking it in cold water. Next, try detergent and lukewarm water. If the stain remains, treat it with a solvent-based spot-treatment stain remover and wash again. The last resort is to soak the item in a solution of water and an oxygen-based, colour-safe bleaching product (or chlorine bleach for white cottons). And if all fails, give up and treat yourself to something new – you deserve it after so much effort!

TOOLS FOR THE JOB

The successful removal of most stains depends upon rapid treatment, so it's a good idea to keep a supply of the most useful stain-removal products. That way, you'll be ready to deal with even the trickiest of stains as soon as they happen.

WHAT TO BUY

A quick glance down the aisles of any supermarket will reveal a bewildering array of cleaning potions, lotions and powders. You certainly don't need all of them, nor would it be practical or economical to fill your home with so many different products. A few carefully chosen specialized items, along with some more general household cleaning materials, will do the job just as well. In this section you'll find a tried-and-tested guide to the top tools for banishing stains. And, because most of us now also worry about the possible damaging effects on the environment of using conventional chemical-based products, a few greener alternatives have been provided too.

Basic tools

To ensure you are ready for any stain emergency, always try to have the following top tools in your cupboard.

BIOLOGICAL WASHING DETERGENT

This is excellent for removing many household stains from cotton fabrics simply by washing them at 40°C; it is also great for many other dirty jobs around the house, such as removing burned-on food from saucepans and brightening up dirty bathtubs.

BLUNT KNIFE

You'll need one of these for gently dry-scraping off any solid or bulky part of a stain before treating it further. On delicate items, take care not to scratch or damage their surface.

CHLORINE BLEACH

While it should always be used with discretion and kept well out of the reach of children, chlorine bleach is still one of the most useful pieces of kit in any stain-

removing arsenal. It can restore white cottons to their original dazzling brightness and remove ugly mould on grout, as well as keep your loo fresh and free of germs. Don't be without it!

CLEAN TOOTHBRUSH AND NAILBRUSH

These are useful for brushing off talc or cornflour that has been used as an absorbent, sprinkled over an oily stain. Only use a soft brush that won't damage delicate fabrics. Old toothbrushes are also perfect for scrubbing nasty mould stains off grout.

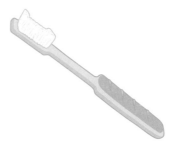

CORNFLOUR OR UNSCENTED TALC

Sprinkle on fatty and oily stains. The powder will absorb some of the grease and can then be removed with a soft brush.

COTTON BUDS

Use these when a light touch is required or the stained area is very small. Dab gently at the stain to lift it.

DETERGENT FOR DELICATES

Some fabrics are just too delicate to withstand normal biological detergents, so always keep a gentle detergent suitable for silk and wool.

GLYCERINE

Glycerine is great for softening and loosening old stains. Dilute it with one to two parts of water and apply to the stain. Allow the item to soak for one hour before washing as normal. Glycerine is available from most pharmacies.

ICE CUBES AND ICE PACKS

These are helpful for removing soft, sticky stains such as candle wax and chewing gum. Apply to the affected area (or if possible, place the entire item in the freezer) and leave until the solid part of the stain is brittle enough to be picked or scraped off with a blunt knife.

MEDICINE DROPPER

A medicine dropper can come in handy for targeting liquid stain removers on very small stains.

METHYLATED SPIRITS

Methylated spirits is a good solvent, and can be used to dissolve greasy stains such as crayon and ballpoint pen; it is essential for curcumin-based stains such as curry and mustard. Use the colourless variety, and remember that it's flammable, so smoking is outlawed. Methylated spirits is not suitable for use on acetate fabrics, and you should be careful when using it on coloured items because it can dissolve some dyes – check for colourfastness on an inconspicuous area first.

NAIL POLISH REMOVER

The only thing that can remove a nail polish stain and even then when the stain is small. Don't use it on acetate fabrics though as it can damage them.

PAPER TOWELS AND CLOTHS

Use white paper towels or clean, white, lint-free cloths for blotting and soaking up moisture in water-based stains. Patterned or coloured towels and cloths could transfer dye and make the stain worse.

SODA OR SPARKLING WATER

Pouring bubbly water on pigment-based spills such as red wine helps to force the stain out of the fabric fibres – handy for emergency action at a dinner party. However, only use makes that are low in salt,

otherwise you may inadvertently end up setting the stain.

STICKY TAPE OR SCOTCH TAPE

Sticky tape is ideal for lifting pollen particles off clothing and carpets. Gently pat the affected area with the tape to remove as much of the debris as possible. This method also works well for removing other dry debris, such as pet hair.

TRAVEL WASH

Used neat and rubbed in with a little warm water and a clean cloth, it's amazingly effective.

WASHING-UP LIQUID

Not just for dishes! Many stains can be removed simply by working in washing-up liquid and rinsing with lots of water.

WET WIPES

Not essential, but useful for getting rid of annoying white deodorant marks on dark-coloured clothing.

WHITE SPIRIT

A good solvent – use it for removing paint and nail varnish.

The specialist products

These favourite, tried-and-tested, specialized products are readily available in supermarkets, but if you have difficulty finding them, consult the Specialist Product Directory, page 183, for suppliers' contact details.

Bissell OxyKIC

An effective spot-treatment carpet cleaner, which combines the power of oxygen and cleaning solvents and is very effective on a large number of stains. If you only have one specialized carpet cleaner in your storecupboard, make sure it's this one.

De.Solv.It

A citrus-based, spot-treatment stain-remover spray, which is good for many types of stain, particularly greasy ones. One of the few products with any effectiveness on difficult mustard stains; it also works well on lipstick, suntan lotion, chewing gum and candle wax. Not recommended for use on silk.

Stain Devils Nos. 1–8

Individually formulated, stain-specific, spot-treatment stain-removers, which are suitable for use on most washable fabrics. Choose the number most suited to the stain type.

Stain Devils Instant Wipes

While not a hundred per cent effective, these handy wipes can provide instant first aid when you're out and about. Keep them in your handbag for those embarrassing moments when lunch ends up down a special outfit. You can then treat the stain appropriately once you get home.

Sticky Stuff Remover

Excellent for dissolving traces left by sticky tape, labels and chewing gum.

WD-40

Not just for squeaky hinges, WD-40 has surprising uses as a stain remover. It's excellent for dissolving chewing gum and traces left by sticky labels, and also works well on greasy stains such as tar, boot polish and lipstick. However, it can leave an oily mark – to prevent this, rub liquid detergent into the affected area before washing the garment as normal. Not suitable for use on silk.

White Wizard

This one's a bit of a wonder product. It's non-toxic, easy to use and suitable for all fabrics. It's effective on a wide range of stains, so if you keep just one specialized product in your stain-removal storecupboard, this is the one to choose.

Wine Away

Another favourite and it does exactly what it says. Friends will be amazed (and grateful!) when the lurid purple mark they've splashed on your best white tablecloth suddenly turns blue before disappearing completely. Wine Away is also good for removing red ink and bloodstains.

ENZYME-BASED PRE-SOAKING AGENTS

(Also known as biological pre-soaking agents.) These work by digesting and breaking down proteins, and are effective on stains such as blood and egg. Don't use them on silk and wool, which are themselves protein-based fibres.

OXYGEN-BASED, COLOUR-SAFE BLEACHING PRODUCTS

These are a good alternative to chlorine bleach. They are less toxic and gentler on delicate fabrics such as silk and wool. A scoop of powder added to the detergent in a normal washload will help to brighten clothing. Many proprietary brands are available – they usually have the word 'oxi' or 'oxy' in their name, so you shouldn't have any difficulty finding one to suit you.

GREENER ALTERNATIVES

These days, we all worry about using too many chemicals in our homes, and the effect that this might have on our health and the environment. Although for certain stains sometimes only the really strong stuff will do, happily, for less stubborn offenders, there are some more natural alternatives that work very well.

For example, did you know that white vinegar is one of the most useful products for carrying out many cleaning tasks, that bicarbonate of soda can be used for more than just cooking, or that washing soda crystals are effective for removing many stains? Our grandmothers used all these ingredients to great effect in keeping their homes clean and there's no reason why you can't do the same, so in this section you will find our top greener alternatives to conventional commercial cleaning products.

Green solutions

If you're uncomfortable using strong chemicals to tackle every stain removal or household task in your home, you'll be pleased to discover that many standard ingredients in your storecupboard can be used as effective cleaning agents. These are our favourites.

BICARBONATE OF SODA

No self-respecting domestic goddess should be without bicarbonate of soda, even if you never bake a cake. It has myriad uses around the home, just a few of which are given here. As a powerful natural deodorizer, it can be placed in the fridge to absorb food smells, and sprinkled on mattresses, carpets and other soft furnishings to remove unpleasant odours such as those left by vomit or sour milk. Bicarbonate of soda also boosts the performance of chlorine bleach – use half a cup of soda to half a cup of bleach (instead of the usual full cup of bleach on its own) for similar results. A scouring paste made from half bicarbonate of soda and half water is excellent for removing stubborn stains from kitchen worktops, sinks, cookers and saucepans. When rubbed into greasy stains on clothing before laundering, a paste made from two parts bicarbonate of soda to one part cream of tartar will help to remove the marks.

DISTILLED WHITE VINEGAR

Vinegar is a wonderful traditional remedy, excellent for removing limescale from a variety of surfaces and for buffing windows to a streak-free shine. It's also a good odour-absorber, and a few drops applied to clothing faded by perspiration will sometimes

restore the colour. However, don't use it on gold-plated fittings or marble surfaces, because it is acidic and can damage them.

LEMON JUICE

Lemon juice is a natural bleaching agent. You can use freshly squeezed juice, but the bottled stuff works just as well. Try removing food stains from chopping boards by rubbing them with lemon juice and leaving them overnight. Lemon juice is also very effective on rust stains, and half a cupful added to a washload will help to brighten whites.

WASHING SODA CRYSTALS

Washing soda has been used in the home for over one hundred years. It is biodegradable, contains no enzymes, phosphates or bleach and can be used on all types of fabric. If you don't want to use strong solvents, enzymes or other stain-removing products, washing soda is a good alternative. It is effective at removing grease, blood, ink, grass, red wine, tea and coffee. Soak the affected garment overnight in a strong solution (follow the

directions given by the manufacturer) before washing as normal. You can use washing soda crystals on many non-fabric stains too, such as burnt pans, discoloured chopping boards and tea-stained cups, and also for an enormous variety of other household cleaning tasks, such as clearing blocked drains or removing mildew from shower curtains. Don't use them on aluminium, though. On fabrics, as with all stain-removing products, always check for colourfastness first. Do not confuse washing soda crystals with caustic soda.

2

Preventive measures

THE BEST WAY OF DEALING WITH STAINS IS TO PREVENT THEM APPEARING IN THE FIRST PLACE

FABRICS AND SOFT FURNISHINGS

If you want to keep your clothes and the soft furnishings around your home in pristine condition, it helps to know how best to look after them. Many an item has been ruined through lack of knowledge about the correct care of textiles. So, in this section you will find out how to treat just about every fabric under the sun, including solving or avoiding common washday problems (such as colour-runs and shrinkage), choosing what sort of detergent to use, how to maintain your wardrobe for maximum protection from dust and pests, and the correct way to store clothes. We've even provided a handy guide to common laundry symbols to help you decipher those fiddly labels on your clothes. And because it's not just your clothes that need care, there's also detailed information on looking after other textiles, such as bedding, carpets and curtains.

A-Z of fabrics and their care

Acetate	Man-made fibre often made into silk-like fabrics such as satin, taffeta and brocade, and linings. Wash in warm water on a programme for delicates. Do not spin. Iron on a cool setting. Avoid using acetone or vinegar to remove stains.
Acrylic	Often used for knitwear, as an alternative to wool or mixed with it. Hand-wash in warm water or use a low-temperature synthetics programme with a short spin. To reduce static, use fabric conditioner in the last rinse. Do not wring, and use a cool iron without steam. Pull back into shape while damp, and dry flat.
Brocade	Heavy, stiff fabric with a raised pattern; often used for soft furnishings and upholstery. Can be made from cotton, silk, viscose or acetate. Dry-clean only.
Broderie anglaise	Traditional, openwork embroidered fabric or lace, available in cotton or polyester. Wash according to fabric type. Wash delicate pieces by hand or in a muslin bag in the washing machine.
Calico	Plain, closely woven cotton, generally unbleached and coarse. Wash as for cotton.
Canvas	Stiff, coarse cotton used for strengthening tailored garments, and for making tents,

handbags and shoes. Sponge or scrub soiled areas with a stain-removal bar. Rinse with cool water.

Seating Scrub with a nailbrush and household soap. Rinse by pouring water through the fabric. Dry naturally, if necessary supporting with a couple of chairs underneath.

Shoes Allow mud to dry before brushing it off. Some canvas shoes can be machine-washed. Use a low-temperature synthetics programme. Alternatively, use an upholstery shampoo or proprietary cleaner for fabric shoes.

Chenille	Heavy fabric made from cotton, viscose, wool or silk, with a soft, velvety pile. Wash according to fabric type, or dry-clean.
Chiffon	Finely woven sheer fabric made from cotton, silk or man-made fibres. Wash according to fabric type, or dry-clean. Do not wring or spin. Iron while still damp, on a cool setting.
Chintz	Tightly woven cotton, generally with a flowery design, used for furnishing fabrics. Some types have a chemical glazed finish. Dry-clean only. Repeated cleaning will remove the glaze.

Corduroy

Cotton or synthetic-mix, woven, ribbed fabric used for clothes and upholstery. Use a synthetics programme with minimum spin. Wash garments such as trousers inside out. Iron on the reverse while damp, using a steam setting. Gently brush up the pile.

Cotton

A natural-fibre fabric, which is available in different weights and qualities. Machine-washable, but may shrink or fade if washed at temperatures over 40°C. Iron while damp, using a steam setting.

Crepe de Chine

Lightweight, slippery fabric traditionally made from silk but now mostly synthetic. Hand-wash according to fibre type. Give it a cold rinse, then roll in a towel to remove moisture. Iron on a cool setting.

Damask

Heavy woven fabric, with shiny thread. Made of silk, cotton, viscose or a combination. Often used for table linen. Wash according to fibre type. Dry-clean heavier items.

Denim

Hard-wearing twilled cotton. If not pre-shrunk, use a cool wash. Turn inside out and wash separately as the colour can run. Iron while still damp, using a high setting, preferably with steam.

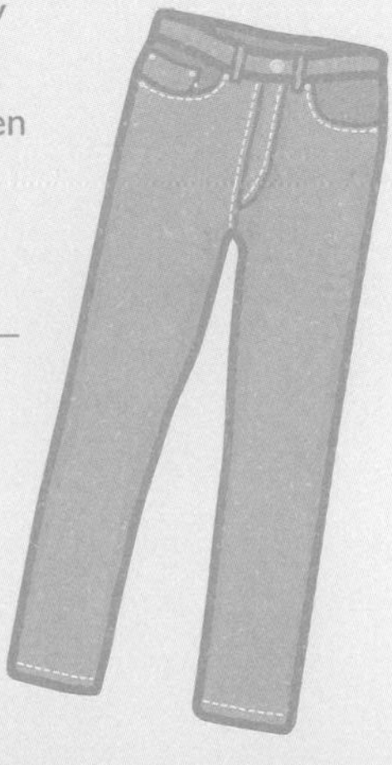

Dralon	Trade name for an acrylic-fibre, velvet-type furnishing fabric. **Upholstery** Brush or vacuum regularly. Clean with a dry-foam upholstery shampoo. **Curtains** Dry-clean. Do not iron. **Stains** Remove **water-based stains** immediately by blotting, then sponge with a weak solution of biological detergent. Rinse and blot dry. For **other stains**, try acetone applied with cotton wool. If in doubt, have the item cleaned professionally.
Elastanes, such as Lycra	A synthetic alternative to rubber, this elastic fibre is usually used in a mixture with cotton or wool. Machine-wash at a low temperature using a programme for delicates, or hand-wash in warm water, rinse and use a short spin or roll in a towel to remove moisture. Do not tumble-dry as this will weaken the elasticity.
Felt	Thick, non-woven material made from matted wool fibres. It should always be dry-cleaned.
Flannel	Woven wool or wool and cotton blend, mainly used for suits. Dry-clean suits and expensive items, otherwise treat as wool.
Fur fabric	Made from polyamide, viscose, cotton, acrylic or polyester. Dry-clean cotton and viscose; wash others as nylon/polyamide, shaking well before allowing to dry naturally. For light soiling, sponge area with a warm solution of non-biological

detergent, rinse and towel dry. Brush straight-pile fabric while still damp. Between washings, brush pile with a medium to hard brush.

Gabardine	Made from wool, cotton or either of these blended with man-made fibres. Often used for coats and suits. Dry-clean only.
Georgette	Fine, sheer fabric made from cotton, silk, wool or man-made fibres. Dry-clean natural fabrics. Wash man-made fabrics according to fibre type.
Grosgrain	Fine, ribbed fabric of silk or man-made blends. Wash according to fibre type, or dry-clean.
Jersey	Stretchy knitted fabric of wool, silk, cotton or man-made fibres. Wash according to fibre type, or dry-clean. Short spin. Dry flat, pulling back into shape while damp. Steam-iron on reverse.
Lace	Cotton, polyester, polyamide or a combination. Wash according to fibre type, using a gentle, non-biological detergent. If machine-washing, place in a muslin bag or a pillowcase. Iron while damp, on the wrong side, pulling into shape. **Antique lace** If not valuable, wash by hand with a detergent for delicates and dry flat. Pin delicate pieces to a padded board covered with cotton and sponge with a mild detergent. Rinse with cold water. Dry-clean precious items or take to a specialist fabric restorer (see Service Providers, page 186).

Leather
(see also nubuck, sheepskin, suede)

Chamois Hand-wash in a warm solution of soapflakes, squeezing to release dirt. Rinse in a warm solution to which 5ml olive oil has been added, in order to retain the soft texture. Squeeze out moisture and pull to shape. Hang to dry away from direct heat. Scrunch up the leather during drying to maintain its flexibility.

Patent Don't let it become very cold or it will crack. Dust with a soft cloth and apply patent-leather dressing when dull. To store, apply a thin layer of petroleum jelly (Vaseline) all over (wipe off when taken out of storage). Use shoe trees or stuff with paper to maintain shape.

Clothing 'Washable' leather clothing should be sponged, never immersed, in water. Treat new or newly cleaned clothes with waterproofing spray. All clothing should be professionally cleaned every three to four years, re-tinted and oiled. You can remove surface soiling from washable leather by gently dabbing the marked area with a sponge dipped in a solution of soapflakes (or liquid detergent) and water. Wipe with a clean, damp cloth and hang to dry. Store leather clothing on a padded hanger in a cotton cover.

Shoes and handbags When new, apply a waterproof protector. Clean shoes regularly with shoe polish to clean and maintain the dye colour, and to cover scuff marks. If they get really wet, dry out at room temperature in a well-ventilated spot. Stuff with paper to help retain the shape, or use a shoe tree. Never dry leather shoes in front of a radiator – it can cause them to crack. Care for handbags as for shoes, but don't use coloured polishes, which can rub off on clothing. To remove grease and oil, coat the stain with a thin layer of rubber adhesive, leave it on for twenty-four hours, then roll off the adhesive. Treat with hide food. Alternatively, use a proprietary shoe-leather cleaner, always testing first for colourfastness.

Linen	A woven fabric made from flax fibres. Give it a hot wash and spin-dry. Hang to dry. Garments with special anti-crease finishes should be dry-cleaned. Iron on the reverse while still damp, using a hot steam iron. Starch occasionally to give the fabric a bit of body.
Moiré	Fabric with an appearance like watered silk. Traditionally made from silk, but now often from synthetics. Heavyweight types are used for furnishings and lighter weights for evening dresses. The surface is easily damaged by water, so dry-clean only. Do not use a steam iron.
Muslin	An open-weave, sheer cotton. Hand-wash carefully in warm water. Do not spin. Dry flat and iron on a medium setting while still damp.
Nubuck	A cow leather, similar to suede, but buffed to a finer velvet pile. To clean, use special nubuck and calfskin cleaners, which require no brushing. Do not use suede shampoos or brushes as they can damage the pile.

Percale	Finely woven cotton or polyester-cotton blend, often used for bedding. Can also be glazed. Wash according to fibre type.
Polyamide, (such as nylon)	Lightweight, non-absorbent, man-made fibre. Elastic and strong even when wet; flame-resistant, but melts instead. Wash in hand-hot water, or on a 40°C delicates cycle in the washing machine. Use fabric conditioner to reduce static. Give it a cold rinse, short spin and leave to drip-dry. Use a cool iron if necessary. Absorbs dye easily, so wash colours separately. Do not bleach. Avoid direct heat and sunlight when drying.
Polyester	Synthetic fibre often combined with cotton. Wash on a 40°C or 50°C synthetics programme with a short spin. Use fabric conditioner in the final rinse. Can be tumble-dried. Treat grease stains immediately by soaking in a solution of biological detergent. Hand-wash pleated items and allow to drip-dry, preferably outside on a clothesline.
Poplin	Closely woven fabric, usually cotton but can also be made from viscose, silk or wool. Wash according to fibre type.
Satin	Smooth fabric with a short nap; made from silk, cotton, polyester, polyamide or acetate. Used for dress fabrics, linings and lingerie. Wash according to fibre type. Iron on the

reverse side while still damp, until dry. Dry-clean heavy satins, or items with a care label that demands it.

Sheepskin

Coats When new, apply a protective spray to help prevent marking. Send to be professionally cleaned regularly. To clean small areas, use a proprietary suede cleaner, but test first.
Rugs Wash at home if the wool pile is quite short, using a solution of soapflakes, or have it cleaned professionally.

Silk

Luxury fibre made from the cocoon of the silkworm. Wash by hand using a non-biological detergent or, if the care label allows, on the delicates cycle in the washing machine. Don't rub or wring the fabric. Use fabric conditioner in the final rinse, then roll up in a clean, dry towel and squeeze lightly to remove water. To improve colourfastness, try soaking (after the final rinse) in a solution of 10ml white vinegar to 3 litres water. Leave for three minutes, then allow to dry. Iron while still slightly damp, using a cool setting. Never wash silk items at home if the care label says dry-clean only and never use enzyme-based detergents.

Suede	**Clothing** Treat new clothes with a waterproof spray to help prevent the colour rubbing off, but test on an inconspicuous area first. Wipe dirty or rain-spotted suede with a clean, damp cloth and allow to dry naturally. Brush frequently with a wire brush or suede block. For serious discolouration, it's best to have the item professionally cleaned. **Shoes** Treat new shoes with a protective suede spray. When necessary, clean with a nailbrush and clean, soapy water. Rinse and blot dry. If shoes get wet, allow them to dry naturally, then use a suede brush to remove dust and raise the pile.
Taffeta	Crisp, closely woven, shiny material made from a variety of fibres including silk, acetate, viscose, polyester or polyamide. Dry-clean. Iron on the reverse side.
Towelling	Looped pile fabric usually made from cotton. Machine-wash on a programme suitable for cotton. Wash dark colours separately. If towels go stiff, soak overnight in a solution of water softener, then machine-wash with maximum detergent. If they are still stiff,

machine wash at the highest temperature with 200ml white distilled vinegar in the detergent dispenser drawer (do not use detergent or fabric softener). Use fabric conditioner every third wash to keep towelling soft.

Tulle	Fine, sheer, net-like fabric of silk, cotton, viscose, polyamide or other fibres; used for evening and bridal wear. Dry-clean silk; hand-wash other fibres following instructions for fibre type. Starch cotton tulle if it becomes limp.
Tweed	Woven woollen fabric available in different weights. Imitations also made in polyester and acrylic. Dry-clean.
Velour	Pile fabric similar to velvet, usually made of acrylic but may consist of other man-made fibres or cotton or silk. Dry-clean or wash according to fibre type. Iron using a cool setting on the reverse side of the fabric.
Velvet	Once a silk or cotton cut pile fabric, but now also made from man-made fibres such as viscose, polyamide and polyester. Treat according to fibre type, or dry-clean. To restore the pile, shake periodically while drying and smooth the pile with a soft cloth or velvet brush. Use steam to remove between-wear creases. Iron with pile face down on a soft cloth or towel.

Viscose
(rayon)

Fibre made from the pulp of eucalyptus and spruce wood, used on its own or in blends. Wash with care at low temperatures. To avoid creasing, use a short spin when washing and do not wring. Iron while damp on a steam setting.

Wool
(including angora, cashmere, mohair)

Hand-wash carefully in warm water or machine-wash on the woollens programme; use a detergent for delicates. Do not rub, wring or twist. Dry flat between two towels, pulling gently to the correct shape while damp. Never tumble-dry. Some wool fabrics are dry-clean only, so always check the care label and never use enzyme-based stain removers.

Wardrobe maintenance

Follow these tips to manage your wardrobe and keep clothes in tip-top condition at all times.

1 KEEP CLOTHES VENTILATED

Cramming clothes into the wardrobe will make them misshapen and encourage mould and mildew. Sort through your things regularly and give away anything you haven't worn for over two years. Make additional space by sorting items according to season and pack away any you don't currently need. Air should be able to circulate freely to help moisture to evaporate, and allow for easier dusting of your clothes. Charcoal briquettes placed in the corners of the wardrobe will help to absorb any excess moisture.

2 KEEP CLOTHES CLEAN

Don't put items that have been worn or are damp into wardrobes or drawers. Wash and dry them first – moisture will attract mould, and stains that are unnoticeable when fresh, such as perspiration,

can oxidize and discolour over time. Human bodily fluids also attract pests such as moths, so keep things clean!

3 KEEP CLOTHES ORGANIZED

Untidy wardrobes and drawers make items hard to find and cleaning more difficult. Fold things before putting them away, this saves on ironing and helps knitwear keep its shape. Remove belts from trousers before hanging to avoid stretching the loops. Use coat hangers made of wood or strong plastic to prevent distortion of the shoulder area.

4 KEEP CLOTHES REPAIRED

Finally, make a point, every six months or so, of inspecting items for loose hems, missing buttons, open seams and holes – repair them yourself or take them to a professional mender.

Storing clothing and textiles

Clothes and textiles that won't be used for a long period should be stored away carefully to prevent damage by moisture and pests. For the best results, follow these guidelines.

Before storing, launder or dry-clean all items. Make sure they are completely dry. Don't iron items that are to be stored, or use starch, as these will make the fibres more brittle and prone to tearing along creases.

Special items can be wrapped in acid-free tissue paper to help prevent creasing and provide further protection. Use cotton gloves to avoid transferring potentially damaging bodily fluids from your hands to the garment.

Avoid using ordinary cardboard or paper boxes; they aren't waterproof, chemicals can leach into your clothing and pests are attracted to protein in the glue used to stick the boxes together. For shorter-term storage, you can use plastic storage boxes, but make sure

they are not completely airtight – the clothes need to breathe, not suffocate! For long-term storage of items such as wedding dresses, the best option is a special acid-free storage box, available from stationers or archiving suppliers (see opposite).

Don't store items in direct contact with wood. All wood contains acids that can damage textiles over a long period of time.

Place the container in a cool place, off the floor and away from damp, sunlight and direct or indirect heat.

If items are being stored for longer than one season, take them out once or twice a year and re-fold them along different lines to prevent stress tears forming on creases. At this time, you should also make a quick check for any other damage that may have occurred.

CARING FOR WEDDING DRESSES, BALLGOWNS AND OTHER PRECIOUS ITEMS

Follow these tips in addition to the standard storage guidelines.

★ Try to fold large wedding dresses and christening gowns 'concertina-style', so that creases are less stiff.

★ Interleave each crease, and pad out bodices and sleeves, with acid-free tissue.

★ Consider having the item professionally vacuum-packed (available at good dry-cleaners) – this should preserve it for at least twenty-five years, but you won't be able to remove the dress during that time, because if the seal is broken the preservative properties will be lost.

★ Make sure that the item is covered by your household contents insurance should any damage befall it.

WARNING

TEXTILE PESTS

Moths and carpet beetles, and their larvae, can be lethal. They love munching textiles, particularly expensive ones such as silk, fur and cashmere. Take action to prevent a trail of destruction being left in your wardrobe:

⚠ Always launder first. Textile pests are attracted by sweat and bodily fluids, food remnants and other perfumed substances, so don't give them the green light by returning soiled or worn clothing to the cupboard.

⚠ Vacuum regularly. They also like dust and hair, so pay particular attention to areas such as along skirting boards, underneath furniture and the insides of wardrobes and drawers.

⚠ Use mothballs or more natural pest repellents, such as lavender and cedar bags, in areas where clothing is kept.

Understanding laundry symbols

SYMBOL	DESCRIPTION	MEANING
	Wash tub	The washing process by machine or hand
	Triangle	Chlorine bleaching
	Iron	Ironing
	Circle	Dry-cleaning
	Circle in square	Tumble-drying (after washing)
	St Andrew's Cross	Do Not

WASHING

COTTON WASH (NO BAR)
A wash tub without a bar indicates that normal (maximum) washing conditions may be used at the appropriate temperature.

WASHING (continued)

 SYNTHETICS WASH (SINGLE BAR)
A single bar beneath the wash tub indicates reduced (medium) washing conditions at the appropriate temperature.

 WOOL WASH (DOUBLE UNDERLINE)
A double underline beneath the wash tub indicates much reduced (minimum) washing conditions, and is designed specifically for machine washable wool products.

Handwash only
Do not machine-wash.

Do not wash

BLEACHING

Any bleach may be used.

Only oxygen bleach/non-chlorine bleach may be used.

Do not use bleach.

TUMBLE-DRYING

May be tumble-dried.

May be tumble-dried with high heat setting.

May be tumble-dried with low heat setting.

Do not tumble-dry.

DRY-CLEANING

Must be dry-cleaned. Letter within the circle and/or bar beneath circle indicates to dry-cleaner the solvent and process to be used.

Do not dry-clean.

IRONING

Iron at cool setting.

Iron at warm setting.

Iron at hot setting.

Do not iron.

Detergent guide

There are so many different detergent products, but do we really need all of them? This short introduction to detergents and other laundry products should help you decide which are best for you.

HOW IS DETERGENT DIFFERENT FROM SOAP?

While soap and detergent basically perform the same function, they are not the same product. Detergents are synthetic products made from petroleum; soap is made from natural fats. Detergents have better cleaning power and are easier to rinse away – they don't leave the familiar ring of 'scum' associated with soap. Another important point about soap is that it will set tannin-based stains, such as tea, coffee or red wine – so if in doubt about the origin of a stain, it's always better to use a detergent.

Biological detergent

Biological detergent contains enzymes that boost cleaning power. It is the best choice for stain removal, but not suitable for prolonged use on silk or wool.

Colour-safe detergent

Contains specially formulated colour protectors designed to help prevent clothes from fading.

Detergent for delicates

Gentler than standard detergents, so more suitable for delicate fabrics such as silk and wool. It does not contain enzymes, brighteners or bleaching agents.

Non-biological detergent

This contains no enzymes and is thought to be less likely to irritate sensitive skin. For this reason, it is also more likely to be free from added fragrances and colourings. However, the lack of enzymes means that it tends to be less effective at stain removal than biological detergent.

POWDER VERSUS LIQUID, GEL OR TABLET DETERGENT

These are all basically the same product – choose according to which you prefer. Powder is usually the cheapest, but is messy to use and you have to measure out the correct dosage yourself. Tablets save you the bother of measuring. Liquids are more expensive, but handy for pre-treating spots and stains prior to washing. They are also less likely to leave those characteristic streaks caused by undissolved powder or tablet detergents.

OTHER INGREDIENTS IN DETERGENT

Builders enhance cleaning action by deactivating the minerals that cause hard water. **Enzymes** break down amino acids in protein-based stains such as blood and egg, so they are more easily removed. **Optical brighteners** are used in detergents to improve the whiteness of fabrics. They work by reflecting light in such a way that the eye is tricked into thinking the washed clothing looks brighter. **Polymers** help to trap and hold dirt and dyes, and prevent them from being redeposited on clothing. **Preservatives** lengthen a product's shelf life. **Fabric conditioners** reduce friction and static, and help to give fabrics a soft, fluffy feel. **Solvents** prevent liquid detergents from separating during storage. **Stabilizers** help maintain enzymes, bleach and suds-making ability, prolonging the product's shelf life. **Surfactants** provide the main cleaning action by improving the wetting ability of water, loosening and removing dirt, then dissolving, emulsifying or suspending it in the wash solution until it is rinsed away.

Washday problem-solver

Here you'll find some handy solutions to common washday problems.

Bobbling on cotton and synthetic blends

Cause	Abrasion of fibres from normal wear.
Cure	Pick off by hand or with sticky tape. Alternatively, use a razor or specific de-fuzzing gadget. De-fuzzing gadgets may remove some of the surface fluffiness of the fabric, which could weaken the garment over time.
Prevention	Difficult to stop, but try washing garments inside out using a delicate wash cycle that has a reduced spin speed. Fabric conditioner may also help. Don't overfill your washing machine.

Dye transfer from other garments (colour-runs)

Cause	Non-colourfast items washed with paler items at too high a temperature.
Cure	For white items, first check that the item does not have a 'do not bleach' symbol. If it does not, soak in a weak solution of household bleach for fifteen minutes. Rinse thoroughly. Repeat as necessary. For coloured items, try using a proprietary colour-run remover, but test on a hidden area first as it may affect the overall colour.
Prevention	Sort washloads carefully. Always wash dark colours separately, and use a low temperature for non-colourfast items.

Excessive creasing

Cause	Incorrect wash programme, overloading the machine, or drying for too long in the tumble-dryer.
Cure	Reduce the wash temperature, or wash smaller loads. Use the synthetics programmes, which have reduced drum agitation and shorter spin cycles at lower speeds.
Prevention	Follow care labelling.

Fabric harshness, particularly in towels

Cause	Over-drying natural fibres; continually not using enough detergent, allowing mineral salts and limescale to build up; or inadequate rinsing of the washload.
Cure	To counter a build-up of mineral salts and limescale, soak the items in a solution of water softener (following the manufacturer's instructions). Also, run the washing machine on empty, using the hottest programme and adding a decalcifying agent to the recommended dose of detergent to remove any calcium build-up within the machine. To remedy inadequate rinsing, wash the item at as high a temperature as possible, without any detergent. Add one cup distilled white vinegar to the dispenser drawer of the machine.
Prevention	Always follow the recommended detergent dosage instructions. Increase the amount if items are heavily soiled. Line-drying outdoors is a good way to keep towels fluffy, as is tumble drying – as long as you take the towels out before they are bone dry. There should be a little natural moisture left in the fibres, which is why radiators aren't ideal because they can over-dry.

Greying of white cottons

Cause	Dirt removed during washing has been redeposited on the clothing as a very thin, uniform layer. This is most likely to occur when insufficient detergent is used.
Cure	Rewash using the maximum dose of detergent and highest wash temperature. Soak in a bleach solution. Rinse thoroughly.
Prevention	Always follow the recommended dosage instructions and wash whites separately.

Rucking of collars and shirt fronts

Cause	Collars and bands have facings containing different sorts of fabrics to stiffen them. These can shrink when washed, causing puckering of the top fabric. Cotton thread used to sew synthetic fabrics can also cause puckering, as the cotton shrinks.
Cure	May be irreversible, but try steam-ironing the garment while still damp and carefully pulling the offending layers back into shape.
Prevention	Dry-clean items or wash in cool water to prevent shrinkage.

White or grey specks or streaks

Cause	Hard water deposits that are present in the local water supply.
Cure	Rewash using the maximum temperature and dosage of detergent. You may also need to soak the washload in a water softener.
Prevention	Increase detergent dosage. In areas where there is very hard water, carry out an empty wash periodically, using just white vinegar or a proprietary washing-machine cleaner, to stop limescale build-up.

Shrinkage and felting of wool

Cause	Too high a wash temperature, excessive agitation, tumble-drying or direct heat when drying.
Cure	You may have some success by re-wetting the item and gently stretching it, but otherwise this one's irreversible.
Prevention	Only machine-wash if the care label gives permission. If in doubt, always hand-wash. Never, ever, tumble-dry wool.

Looking after soft furnishings

Here you can find advice on the cleaning and care of all sorts of soft furnishings around the home.

BEDDING

Who wants to get into a stinky bed? We spend around eight hours asleep every night, so why not make yours as comfortable as possible. There are few things as satisfying as sinking into crisp, clean sheets at the end of a long working day, knowing you'll be able to sleep soundly and dream sweetly.

Blankets

Usually made from wool, but cotton and synthetics are available. Most wool blankets should be dry-cleaned. Synthetics and cottons are usually machine-washable. Launder at least once a year and dry naturally away from direct heat. Rest blankets occasionally to prolong their life. When not in use, wash and dry thoroughly and store in a breathable polythene bag in a cool cupboard.

Duvets

Never dry-clean feather duvets. Wash in a large launderette machine, checking first that there are no holes or weak points in the casing fabric. If so, repair and patch first. Use one-third of the usual amount of detergent. Shake out while damp to stop the item going lumpy, then dry thoroughly and leave out to air for a day.

Spills and stains Mop up spills immediately to stop them soaking through to the filling. If the casing has become stained, ease the filling away from that area and tie it off with an elastic band or string. Sponge this area first with cold water, then with a mild detergent solution or other appropriate stain treatment – don't over-wet it.

Maintenance Air frequently to keep the filling fluffy and dry. Shake regularly to redistribute the filling. Vacuum occasionally, using the lowest setting on the machine.

Mattresses

Mattresses should be turned regularly, unless the manufacturer's care label says otherwise. This helps to ensure even wear and maintain the shape of the mattress. Vacuum every month, using low suction, and paying particular attention to areas such as underneath buttons and along piping – you'll be horrified by the amount of dust and other gunk that can accumulate there! Consider buying separate mattress covers, which help protect the mattress's surface, and can be removed for washing every couple of months.

Spills and stains Dried stains are difficult to remove. Tip the mattress on its side and sponge with cold water – don't over-wet it. Blot thoroughly and spot-treat with carpet or upholstery shampoo. Rinse and blot dry. For urine or other stinky stains, add a few drops of disinfectant to the rinsing water. Persistent odours can sometimes be eliminated by sprinkling bicarbonate of soda over the affected area, leaving it for a few hours, then vacuuming it off.

Pillows

Pillows take a real battering. Our heads rest on them for around eight hours a night, depositing dead skin, sweat, dribble and other nasty stuff! They should be washed at least twice a year to remove not only debris, but also the dust mites that enjoy feeding on it. Many pillows, even feather ones, can be machine-washed. Check the label, then follow the instructions given for duvets and quilts. Don't dry-clean because the chemicals are difficult to remove and you certainly don't want to be breathing in toxic fumes during the night.

WARNING

A NOTE ON DUST MITES

Dust mites love the bedroom. Moisture, heat and dead skin from your body seep into bedding and provide mites with the perfect living environment. You can't see them, but there are estimated to be around two million dust mites in the average mattress. As they digest the food we provide, each one deposits around twenty excrement pellets per day into the bed. This can be harmful to your health and is a known trigger for allergies; it can cause symptoms such as asthma, eczema, itchy eyes and a running nose. To keep dust mites at bay:

⚠ Turn mattresses regularly and vacuum thoroughly.

⚠ Launder bed linen at least once each week, at 60°C or higher. Cooler washing temperatures will remove allergens, but won't kill the mites. If your bed linen can't take such high temperatures, placing it in the freezer overnight before washing will do the trick.

⚠ Keep humidity and heat below levels that support mites. Leave a window open at night and air the bedding and the room in the morning.

CARPETS, CURTAINS AND OTHER SOFT UPHOLSTERY

Soft furnishings need looking after too, to prevent them from looking drab and dull. A few minutes' regular maintenance will help keep them in excellent condition, and make them last for longer.

Carpets

Carpets provide a lovely, warm, insulated feeling in a home, but can be a magnet for dust and pests such as moths, mites and carpet beetles. Vacuum them regularly to remove embedded dirt and grit, which can damage fibres. Remove footwear at the front door to prevent debris from outside being trampled across the carpets. Use rests to protect pile from castors and heavy furniture. Indentations can be removed by placing an ice cube on the spot, allowing it to melt, then gently teasing up the pile with a soft brush. Have carpets cleaned professionally once a year, especially if there are allergy sufferers in the house. When using any stain-removers, always ensure you rinse out thoroughly; if traces are left behind this may attract dirt.

Curtains and other window dressings

Curtains should be vacuumed weekly from top to bottom on a low setting, using the upholstery tool. Pay particular attention to the top, where dust collects, and the hem, where dirt from the floor is more likely to transfer to the curtain. Roller blinds can be dusted with a soft brush, or by vacuuming with the upholstery tool. To clean venetian blinds, wear white cotton gloves and run your fingers over the slats – much less fiddly than using a duster! Some curtain fabrics can be machine-washed, but velvet, velour, chenille, tapestry, brocade, wool, silk and interlined curtains should be dry-cleaned. Whatever the fabric, wash curtains thoroughly or clean them at least every couple of years, otherwise dirt will start to rot the fibres. Keep window ledges free from dust and mildew.

STEP BY STEP
CURTAIN CLEANING
(WASHABLE FABRICS)

 Before you start, remove all hooks and curtain weights and loosen the heading tape. Let down the hem if the fabric is likely to shrink slightly. Shake to remove dust.

 Soak the curtains in cold water first. Then wash carefully, according to the type of fabric. If hand-washing, make sure the detergent is thoroughly dissolved before immersing the curtains. Do not rub or wring.

3 Rinse thoroughly. Squeeze out as much water as possible, or use a short spin. If machine-washing, use a programme for delicates.

4 Iron the curtains while still damp. Work lengthways, on the wrong side, stretching the fabric gently to stop the seams puckering. Hang the curtains while slightly damp so they drop to the right length.

 Clean curtain tracks, windows and sills before putting the curtains back.

Soft upholstery

Dust often, using the brush attachment and crevice tool of the vacuum cleaner, otherwise crumbs and other nasty bits and pieces can rub up against the fabric where you sit and gradually wear away the weave and pile. Pet hairs can be removed by wrapping your fingers in sticky tape and applying to the affected areas. Turn removable cushions weekly to ensure even wear, and plump them back into shape at the end of an evening's sitting. Wash or dry-clean loose covers according to fabric type. If covers cannot be removed, have them cleaned professionally.

Care Position upholstery away from direct sunlight to stop it fading. Use arm covers and headrests to protect upholstery from perspiration and other fluids, which can affect the long-term durability of fabric. Don't sit on light-coloured suites, especially pale leathers, wearing denim or non-colourfast clothing – dye from clothing can transfer to the upholstery and permanently discolour it. Remove spots and stains as soon as possible, using a proprietary carpet or upholstery cleaner.

Special directions for leather
Dust regularly and occasionally apply hide food or saddle soap (available from furniture outlets or department stores) to prevent the leather from drying out, and to protect against stains. Remove all-over grime by wiping with a soft, damp cloth. Site leather furniture away from radiators or other direct heat, as these can cause it to crack.

HOUSEHOLD FITTINGS AND SURFACES

Unfortunately, stains and other cleaning mishaps don't just occur on textiles. Your entire home needs regular attention to keep it hygienic and looking its best. In this section you will find out how to look after bathroom and kitchen fittings including appliances, and flooring, wall coverings and windows around the house. Bathrooms and kitchens are particularly important because the moisture, food and human waste found in them provide a perfect breeding ground for all sorts of nasties to develop. To prevent moulds, rust and limescale from taking over, you need to put on the rubber gloves and get to work! If you take a few minutes each day to do little tasks such as wiping down surfaces or clearing away clutter, it needn't be a hassle. Follow our tips and with a bit of effort and planning, you'll be able to develop a regime that keeps everything in top condition without having to spend every spare minute cleaning.

Bathrooms

Left unattended, even for short periods, a bathroom will quickly become a health hazard, with clogged plugholes, limescale build-up on taps, and mould and mildew on surfaces. A few minutes of daily maintenance in the bathroom will keep it sparkling and safe.

BATHS
Acrylic and fibreglass

Rinse and dry the bath after every use to deter stains and limescale. Clean regularly with an all-purpose bathroom cleaner to prevent dirt and scum accumulating. Use a nylon bristle brush on stubborn marks, but not an abrasive cleaner. In hard water areas, use a limescale cleaner, especially around the taps. Rub any scratches gently with metal polish, then clean the bath.

Enamel-coated cast iron or steel

Clean as for acrylic baths, but use only products recommended for this type of surface, and a soft cloth. Products with anti-limescale ingredients may cause enamel to dull. Instead, remove limescale with a solution of half white vinegar and half water, applied with a soft cloth – avoid getting vinegar on other parts of the bath, eg taps. Rinse thoroughly and dry. Reduce rust stains by rubbing them with lemon juice and salt. If the bath is very old, it may not be able to take modern cleaners, so test products on a small area first. If the bath has become matt, or damaged by scale deposits, have it professionally cleaned and polished, but if the damage is severe, you may need to have it completely resurfaced. This is expensive, so it's probably more economical to buy a new one.

Whirlpool and spa baths

It is important to clean out scum in the pipework. Once a week, fill the bath with water and add a cleaning agent (the recommended product or a cup of baby-bottle sterilizing fluid). Allow to circulate for five minutes. Empty the bath, refill with clean water and leave to circulate for a further five minutes to rinse.

GLEAMING BATHROOMS

Maintenance tips for a clean, safe bathroom:

★ Toothbrush mugs are a haven for all sorts of nasty bacteria. Clean them thoroughly at least once a week.

★ Once a month, pour a kettle of boiling water over a cup of washing soda crystals scattered around each plughole. This will help clear grease and soap scum, banish odours and leave drains running freely.

★ Replace cleaning cloths regularly, or clean and soak in a disinfectant or bleach solution at least once a week. Keep cloths used for the toilet in a separate place.

★ Buff mirrors with a little white vinegar and paper towels for a sparkling, smear-free finish.

★ After using the bathroom, leave a window open or run the extractor fan to ventilate it and discourage mould from developing.

★ If the bath is very dirty, fill it with warm water and a couple of scoops of biological washing powder, and leave to soak overnight.

BASINS

Rinse out and dry after each use. Clean with an all-purpose bathroom cleaner and wipe with a damp cloth. Make sure the plughole is rinsed thoroughly, as some cleaners can damage its coating. Buff brass or gold-plated plugholes after use to prevent discolouration.

GROUT AND SEALANT

To remove mould, use a fungicidal bathroom spray, and spray regularly to prevent regrowth. Scrub discoloured grout with an old toothbrush dipped in a solution of one part bleach to four parts water.

SHOWERS

After showering, leave the door or curtain open – this helps prevent the humid atmosphere that encourages mould to grow. Wipe down wet tiles with a plastic-bladed window wiper to stop watermarks from forming. Scrub the shower tray with all-purpose bathroom cleaner, rinse and wipe dry. In hard water areas, use a limescale remover once a week.

Shower curtains and screens

Nylon shower curtains can be removed and put into the washing machine – do this every month to stop mildew and soap scum building up. Remove the curtain before the spin cycle and hang immediately so that creases can drop out. If the curtain is not machine-washable, clean it in a bathful of warm water containing a cup of biological detergent. Soak heavily stained curtains in a weak solution of bleach to remove mould stains. Clean glass screens with a sponge and a solution of water and white vinegar. On folding shower screens, pay particular attention to hinged areas, which can get very grubby.

Showerheads

Descale once a month with a liquid descaler and an old toothbrush. Alternatively, steep in a solution of half white vinegar and half water and leave for two hours (never use this method on gold-plated taps: it can damage their finish). Finally, use a needle to de-clog any spray holes that are still blocked.

TAPS

Products such as toothpaste can damage the coating on taps, particularly those with a gold or brass finish. Ideally, you should wipe taps and buff them dry after every use. Clean regularly with a solution of washing-up liquid, rinse and dry. Never use abrasive cleaners on taps. To remove limescale deposits, soak a cloth in a proprietary descaler, or a solution of equal parts white vinegar and water (don't use this method on plated taps). Wrap it around the tap, leave for a few hours, then remove the cloth, rinse the tap and dry.

TOILET

To keep the toilet bowl clean, use a toilet brush and bathroom cleaner with added disinfectant, or fit an in-cistern cleaner to release cleaner or bleach with every flush. Pay particular attention to the areas under the rim. Wipe down the outside of the bowl and the cistern with an all-purpose bathroom cleaner. Don't forget to do the toilet handle – people rarely clean their hands before flushing and this is an area that collects lots of bacteria. Neutralize odours by pouring a cup of washing soda crystals or bicarbonate of soda down the bowl once a week. Washing soda will also clear limescale from around the inside of the bowl: sprinkle in some crystals, leave to soak overnight, then flush away in the morning.

Toilet brushes

These can be nasty things – they collect faeces and are usually left sitting around in a dirty container full of bacteria-harbouring water. Clean yours at least once a week! Put the brush in the toilet bowl, pour some bleach into the water, then leave the brush to stand in it for a few minutes. In the meantime, fill the brush container with hot, soapy water to which a few drops of bleach have been added, swish it around and empty the dirty water away – the best place is down the toilet (after you have removed the brush, of course). Flush clean water over the brush and return it to the container. Buy a new toilet brush at least once a year.

Kitchens

The kitchen is the heart of the home and requires lots of tender, loving care to keep it in tip-top condition. Greasy worktops, overflowing rubbish bins and a cache of food that is past its sell-by date should be dealt with promptly to ensure that your kitchen doesn't become a no-go zone.

WORKTOPS

Keep all kitchen worktops spotlessly clean. Move surface appliances regularly and wash the areas where they have been standing – even the smallest scrap of food is a magnet for pests, so don't leave crumbs or food debris scattered across the worktops.

Ceramic tiles

Treat as for other worktops below. Clean dirty grout with a toothbrush and a solution made of one part bleach to four parts water. Wipe over with a damp cloth and allow to dry.

Natural solid surfaces (such as granite), laminates and man-made solid surfaces

Wipe down with hot, soapy water, or use an all-purpose cleaner with added disinfectant. Use a clean cloth or paper towels to dry. Remove stains by scrubbing gently with a cream cleaner, such as Cif, or a paste made of bicarbonate of soda and water. On textured surfaces, use a nylon bristle brush to get into the grain.

Stainless steel

To remove fingermarks, put a dab of cooking or baby oil on a clean cloth and rub the whole surface, concentrating on marked areas. For thorough cleaning, wash stainless steel with a solution of washing-up liquid and buff dry with a soft cloth.

Wood

Treat as other natural surfaces. Reoil kitchen worktops every three months or so to keep them stain- and water-resistant.

A SPOT-FREE KITCHEN

Maintenance tips for a healthy, sweet-smelling kitchen:

★ Change kitchen cloths at least twice a week or sterilize them daily by soaking in a bleach solution. Keep separate cloths for washing dishes and for wiping up spills on surfaces.

★ To keep chopping boards stain-free and hygienic, always scrub them in hot, soapy water. Rinse under hot running water or, better still, pour boiling water over them to sterilize, and dry thoroughly.

★ If carrot or curry stains on the food processor bowl don't come out with normal washing, try wiping the bowl with kitchen paper moistened with vegetable oil, then washing in hot soapy water. This will often remove the marks.

★ Remove smells from a microwave oven by placing lemon slices in a bowl of water inside the oven and heating on high power until boiling, then heat for twenty minutes on medium power so steam passes through the vents.

DISHWASHERS

How on earth did we ever manage without dishwashers? They're a wonderful invention, but do need a little attention to keep them in good working order. Before cleaning, switch off the electricity supply. Clean filters after each use. Spray arms should be cleaned in a solution of washing-up liquid – run water through the inlet of each spray arm to ensure that holes are not blocked with food debris. To banish unpleasant smells coming from the dishwasher, sprinkle a couple of tablespoons of bicarbonate of soda on the bottom of the machine before running a load. To keep limescale and soap scum build-up at bay, periodically run a cup of white vinegar through the machine on a normal cycle. Alternatively, use one of the proprietary dishwasher-cleaning products that are available.

HOBS

If possible, hobs should be cleaned immediately after each use, while dirt is still fresh and easy to remove with a quick wipe. Don't forget to wipe down knobs and any other areas your sticky hands may have been!

Glass-topped (including ceramic, halogen and induction)

Wipe up spills immediately, especially sugar, which can crystallize and damage the hob. Use a specialized hob cleaner to remove light soiling. Stubborn stains and burned-on deposits should be removed with a special hob scraper, which will not damage the glass. To prevent scratches, always lift pans when moving them across the hob, and check that the bases of pans are clean and dry.

Gas

Some pan supports and spillage wells are dishwasher-safe. Otherwise, use a cream cleaner and a damp cloth.

OVENS

Many otherwise sparkling kitchens hide a dirty little secret! How many of us are guilty of neglecting the oven simply because we can't see inside? It's a job we all hate, but, like it or not, it does need to be cleaned from top to bottom every now and again. Make the job easier in advance by wiping the interior surfaces with paper towels after each use, and line the base either with a piece of foil or one of those easy-clean oven sheets you can buy in most kitchen shops. For heavy-duty cleaning, always follow the manufacturer's instructions, or use a specialized oven cleaner, making sure it does not come into contact with stay-clean linings. These products can be toxic, so always wear rubber gloves and make sure the room is well ventilated. To make cleaning easier, place a heat-resistant bowl of water in the oven and

heat on a high temperature for twenty minutes. This will help loosen dirt and grease.

Oven doors

Remove cooked-on deposits with a metal spatula or ceramic hob scraper, then use a spray-on oven cleaner. A paste made from bicarbonate of soda and water also works well. If the glass is removable, soak it in a solution of biological detergent to remove grime.

Oven shelves

Clean them in the dishwasher if they'll fit. If not, soak them in the bathtub in a solution of biological washing detergent and water. Any remaining deposits can be removed by scrubbing with a mild abrasive cleaner or soap-impregnated pad.

REFRIGERATORS AND FREEZERS

Get into the habit of checking the contents of the fridge and freezer regularly. If you don't, unpleasant things happen. Shelves become sticky with festering food and old spillages, and furry green moulds start appearing on long-forgotten

items. At least once a week, check the date labels and throw out anything past its sell-by date. This is also a good time to wipe shelves and drawers, and mop up any spills.

To clean a fridge thoroughly

Turn the fridge off. Remove all the food and put perishable items in a cool place. Run shelves and drawers through the dishwasher, or clean in hot, soapy water. Pull out the fridge and wipe all interior and exterior surfaces to remove grease and marks, and dry with a soft cloth. Don't forget to clean inside the folds of the door seal – lots of crumbs and other debris collect there. While the fridge is away from the wall, vacuum up any dust that has settled on the

condenser coil on the back – this helps it to work more efficiently. Place a bowl of bicarbonate of soda inside the fridge to absorb any unpleasant smells – this should be replaced every month.

Defrosting the freezer

Do this as soon as the ice inside reaches a thickness of around 3cm. Turn the freezer off and go through its contents. Throw away anything you are unlikely to use. It's a good idea to use a marker pen to label when the food went into the freezer and then throw the food after 1–3 months depending on its star rating. Be ruthless. Put the remaining items in a coolbox. Stand bowls of hot water on tea towels inside the freezer to hasten the defrosting process and change them as they cool. Don't be tempted to use anything sharp to scrape at the ice: you run the risk of damaging the cooling elements. While the ice is defrosting, clean all the shelves and drawers. When the ice has melted, mop up water with tea towels, then wipe the freezer dry and replace its contents. Don't forget to switch the freezer back on.

SINKS

The sink is a vital part of your kitchen equipment. So many tasks are performed in or around it – preparing food, washing dishes and hands, rinsing out paintbrushes, even cleaning mud off shoes. It's a magnet for dirt and grease, so you need to be vigilant about keeping it clean. However, modern sinks are made from such a range of materials that it can be difficult to know where to begin. Start with the sink's manufacturer. Many of them sell their own cleaning products and can send you specific instructions on caring for the sink.

Coloured and composite sinks

Wipe with a damp cloth and washing-up liquid solution or an anti-bacterial spray cleaner. For thorough cleaning, use a neat multi-purpose liquid or cream cleaner, rinse and dry. If you live in a hard water area, use a limescale cleaner once a week. Avoid using a plastic washing-up bowl as this can trap grit underneath and cause scratching. Putting neat bleach down the plughole can cause staining, so only use it diluted.

Don't allow tea, coffee or other highly coloured foods to dry on the sink as they can stain. Soak stubborn stains in a solution of biological washing detergent or well-diluted household bleach. Plugholes and overflows get dirty too – use a bottlebrush to give them a good scrub once a week.

Enamel sinks

Treat as for coloured and composite sinks, but limescale removers are not recommended. To remove limescale, try using a plastic scourer, neat washing-up liquid and plenty of elbow grease.

Stainless-steel sinks

Treat as for coloured and composites.

TAPS

Don't overlook the taps. Give them a regular wipe with detergent solution to remove grime and buff dry to prevent water spots.

TUMBLE-DRYERS

Tumble-drying gets the job done so much faster, but you must look after your machine to get the best out of it. Make sure all vents and vent pipes are unobstructed and free of kinks. Clean the filter after every use – the dust and lint that collect can be a fire hazard. If it's a condenser model, empty the water reservoir after every use – it's usually located at the top or bottom of the machine.

WASHING MACHINES

In times past, doing the washing was jolly hard work, involving lots of pounding, rubbing and wringing. Thankfully, automatic washing machines have changed all that. Modern machines aren't infallible though, so unless you want to go back to the bad old days, look after yours properly. Wipe out detergent drawers with a damp cloth after each use to keep them free of soap build-up. Every couple of months, pull out the entire drawer and clean it thoroughly in hot, soapy water. While the drawer is out, wipe down the drawer recess with a damp cloth (unplug the machine first). Check and clean drain filters regularly – you'll be amazed by the amount of fluff that collects there. Inspect hoses for signs of wear or weakness. Most manufacturers recommend changing hoses every five years. Keep the exterior of the machine free of dust, which can be a fire hazard. Leaving the machine door slightly ajar when not in use will allow water to evaporate and discourage moulds from growing on the rubber seal.

Flooring (hard)

Vacuum or sweep hard floors regularly to prevent the surface being scratched by grit (and if shoes are removed at the front door it will help to stop dirt from being tracked in). If possible, follow the manufacturer's recommendations for sealants and polishes. See page 68 for information on carpet care.

CORK

Wipe factory-sealed cork tiles with a damp mop, using a solution of washing-up liquid. To provide an extra layer of protection, especially in high-traffic areas such as the bathroom and kitchen, apply an acrylic or polyurethane sealant. Never over-wet and take care not to damage the seal or protective coatings by dragging appliances or furniture over the floor.

LAMINATE

Vacuum, dust or wipe with a lightly dampened mop – never use soap-based detergents or other polishes as they can leave a dull film on the floor, and avoid over-wetting. Don't use wax polish: it will make the floor too slippery. To remove marks and stains, use a dilute solution of water and vinegar.

Never be tempted to use abrasive cleaners, including nylon scouring pads and steel wool, which can scratch. Stubborn marks such as shoe polish can be removed with nail polish remover containing acetone, or other mild solvents – WD-40 also works well. To protect the floor, put felt pads underneath furniture legs, and drip trays under plant pots.

LINOLEUM

Sweep or vacuum to remove grit and dust. Clean with a mop or cloth dampened with a solution of detergent or floor cleaner. Use water sparingly. Rinse after washing. Stubborn marks can be removed by rubbing lightly with a dampened fine nylon pad.

STONE

As it is susceptible to staining, stone should always be protected with a resin sealant. To clean sealed stone, vacuum it thoroughly, then mop with a mild detergent solution. To remove grease or oil, use a proprietary spot-treatment stain remover for stone.

CERAMIC AND QUARRY TILES

These need minimal maintenance. Sweep and wash with a mild detergent solution. Rinse with clear water. Never use wax polish – the tiles will become slippery.

TERRACOTTA TILES

For the first year after installation, terracotta tiles mature. Most suppliers stock a special cleaner, sealant and polish, so use recommended products.

VINYL

Sweep with a soft brush, or vacuum, then wipe with a damp mop, using a mild detergent. Rinse thoroughly after wiping. To remove scuff marks, use a cloth dipped in neat washing-up liquid or white spirit, then rinse off.

WOOD

Sealed floors need only to be swept and damp-mopped. Do not use too much water or the wood could swell and split. Unsealed and waxed floors should be swept regularly and occasionally repolished. Use wax sparingly, as an excess will leave a tacky surface and attract dirt. Buff well. If worn patches appear on the surface, apply a non-slip floor polish. On a waxed floor, polish and dirt builds up over time and the only way to clean it is to remove the wax and start again. Use a cloth moistened with white spirit. Let it soak in, and as the wax and dirt begin to dissolve, wipe away with crumpled newspaper. Scrub obstinate parts by hand, or with abrasive pads on a floor polisher. When polish has been removed, damp-mop with clean water. Allow to dry completely before applying new polish, working on small sections at a time. Never varnish a waxed floor – it won't dry!

Scuff marks on skirting boards
Squirt with WD-40 and wipe away with a soft cloth.

Wall coverings

Wall coverings are often delicate, particularly paper, so always test cleaning methods on an inconspicuous area first. Wipe with a very lightly dampened sponge, dipped in a solution of washing-up liquid. Don't rub hard or you may damage the surface. To make cleaning easier, consider using washable paper or paint.

PAINTWORK

Heavily soiled paintwork can be washed with a sugar soap solution, and rinsed with clear water. Marks such as ballpoint pen, crayon and coloured pencil can often be removed by first rubbing gently with a soft eraser, then dabbing with a cotton bud dipped in White Wizard (see Specialist Product Directory, page 183). Use the soft brush attachment of your vacuum cleaner to remove dust and cobwebs.

FABRICS

Fabric wall coverings tend to be fragile, so always follow the manufacturer's care and cleaning instructions. Don't put fabric coverings up in areas where there is likely to be continual touching with hands. Dust occasionally with a dry cloth or the soft brush attachment of the vacuum cleaner.

WALLPAPER

Fingermark Try rubbing the area gently with a balled-up piece of fresh white bread.

Rips and tears in patterned paper Tear, rather than cut, a suitably sized piece out of leftover paper (ragged edges show less than smooth). Spread the back with thin wallpaper paste to cover. Position the patch over the torn area to match the pattern as well as you can. Smooth down with a clean damp cloth and leave to dry.

Windows

Take down net curtains and blinds. Clear windows and sills. Avoid cleaning windows on very sunny days – the heat will make the glass dry too quickly and cause smears.

Frame

Clean off mildew with an old rag dipped in a proprietary fungicide or a solution of bleach.

Glass

Use a proprietary window cleaner or mix your own with a solution of one part white vinegar to nine parts water. Use a lint-free cloth or chamois leather. Buff the window dry with crumpled newspaper.

Sill

Check sills regularly for rot, and replace any crumbling putty with the correct type for either timber or metal. Repaint as necessary.

Metal window screens

In erasable pencil, write a number on each window. Write a corresponding number on the screen before removing it from the window so you know which screen goes back where. Remove the screens and dust the mesh and frame with the soft brush attachment of a vacuum cleaner. Scrub both sides of the screen with a stiff brush dipped in detergent solution (if you are doing this in the bathtub, line it with towels to prevent scratching the finish). Rinse using a shower attachment or the fine spray nozzle of a hosepipe. Leave to dry thoroughly in a sunny spot before refitting to the window.

HOUSEHOLD ITEMS

We all want to look after treasured items so they last for as long as possible. The cutlery set that was a wedding gift from your parents, the dinner service that cost a bomb and took years of saving to acquire, or the crystal brought back from a trip abroad. These are the things that partly make us who we are and bring us happiness and fond memories over the years. However, all of them need to be handled lovingly if they are to last – neglect can lead to rusting, scratching and tarnishing or all sorts of other unhappy outcomes. In this section you will find the best ways to care for favourite glassware, crockery and cutlery, metalware and many other precious household items.

Kitchenware

Crockery and cutlery can be prone to chipping, scratching, rusting and staining, but if you take a few precautions in their handling, you should be able to avoid or rectify most problems quite easily.

CROCKERY

It's best to wash all dirty dishes as soon as possible. If you're busy with guests, at least rinse the dishes under a hot tap to stop food debris hardening or staining. Thankfully, most china can be put in the dishwasher, with the exception of hand-painted and antique pieces, and those with a metallic trim. Load the dishwasher so pieces do not touch one another, to counter the risk of chipping.

Hand-washing

Use a hot solution of washing-up liquid and a soft brush or sponge. Avoid scouring pads, harsh abrasives and bleach, which can damage the surface or dull patterns. Rinse in clean hot water, drain, then dry with a clean tea towel. Don't stack wet pieces on top of one another as the footing is often unglazed and may scratch the piece underneath.

CUTLERY

For some reason, washing cutlery always seems to be the least favourite part of doing the washing-up. As with crockery though, at least most of it can go straight into the dishwasher. See Cutlery Stains on page 113.

Stainless steel

This can usually go in the dishwasher, but rinse off food deposits first by hand, and remove as soon as the dishwasher cycle has ended. Never use the rinse and hold cycle, as the humid atmosphere may cause 'rust' marks. Polish occasionally with a proprietary stainless-steel cleaner to maintain a mirror-like finish. Wash thoroughly after polishing.

Glassware

To obtain maximum life and performance from your treasured crystal and glassware, careful handling is required. Treat it well and you'll be rewarded with years of happy drinking. If you abuse it, you'll just have to face the scratched and cloudy consequences!

GLASSES

For best results, wash glasses by hand in warm water and washing-up liquid. Remove any sharp jewellery that could scratch the items. Rinse the glasses in hot water containing a few drops of vinegar for added shine. Drain and dry with a soft, lint-free cloth, preferably linen.

DECANTERS AND CARAFES

To remove stains in the base, fill with a warm solution of biological washing detergent and leave to soak. If the stain is stubborn, try adding two tablespoons of rice to the liquid and gently swirl it around to help loosen the dirt. After cleaning, rinse the decanter or carafe thoroughly in warm water. Stand it upside down in a wide-necked jug to drain and make sure it is completely dry before storing it.

LEAD CRYSTAL

Always hand-wash as for glassware. Dishwashers can scratch crystal.

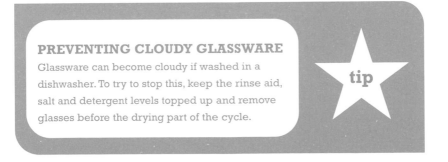

PREVENTING CLOUDY GLASSWARE

Glassware can become cloudy if washed in a dishwasher. To try to stop this, keep the rinse aid, salt and detergent levels topped up and remove glasses before the drying part of the cycle.

tip

Pans

Treated well, decent-quality pans will last you a lifetime. Always follow the manufacturer's instructions if possible, or use the guidelines given here.

Aluminium

Anodized and uncoated aluminium pans should never be washed in a dishwasher. Always hand-wash in plain, soapy water. If uncoated aluminium develops a black tarnish, remove it by boiling up acidic foods such as cut lemon in water.

Cast iron

Always wash uncoated iron pans by hand. Dry thoroughly and brush with a thin layer of vegetable oil to prevent rusting.

Copper

Wash in a solution of washing-up liquid. Polish as for brass (see Metalware opposite).

Glass ceramic

Usually dishwasher-safe. Remove burnt-on food by soaking the pan in a warm solution of washing-up liquid, then use a nylon scourer.

Non-stick coatings

Wash, rinse and dry new pans before use. The non-stick coating may need to be 'seasoned' by brushing the interior with a thin layer of vegetable oil. Re-season after dishwashing (check instructions on pan for dishwashing guidelines). Remove burnt-on food deposits with a scourer specifically for non-stick surfaces. Don't use metal kitchen implements on non-stick pans.

Stainless steel

Wash by hand or in a dishwasher. Rainbow markings may develop over time, but can usually be removed with a proprietary stainless-steel polish or cleaner. Pans subjected to too high a heat may develop brown marks on the exterior, which can also be removed with stainless-steel polish.

Metalware

Wash brass, copper, pewter and silver or silver plate in a warm solution of washing-up liquid and water. Rinse in hot water and dry with a soft cloth.

Brass and copper

After washing, use one of the following polishing methods. If you don't want to buy a special cleaner, try rubbing the surface with half a lemon dipped in salt. Rinse and buff dry with a soft cloth. This method, however, tends to lighten copper and bring out the orange colour. Alternatively, apply a proprietary cream or liquid with a soft cloth and buff before the polish is completely dry. Some brands can be rinsed off with water and are ideal for intricate pieces. For heavier tarnishing, use copper or brass wadding impregnated with polish. This is messy and requires elbow grease. Do not use too frequently as it is quite abrasive.

Pewter

Never use harsh polish. If the item is heavily tarnished, use a proprietary silver cleaner.

Silver

For dusting, use impregnated silver polishing cloths or mitts. Silver is a soft metal, so don't rub too hard. Use straight, even strokes – never rub silver crosswise or with a rotary movement. For polishing, use one of the following methods. A cream or liquid polish is often recommended by manufacturers of fine silver services – these products are ideal for moderately tarnished items. Allow to dry to a fine, powdery deposit, then buff with a soft, dry cloth. Foaming paste is ideal for cutlery, and for covering larger areas such as platters. Apply the paste with a damp sponge and lather to a foam. Rinse in water and dry thoroughly. Sprays are good for covering large areas; wadding is available for heavily tarnished items. See the guidelines for brass and copper (left).

Wooden furniture

The best way to stop furniture being spoiled is to protect it. Use coasters and mats for glasses and tableware, to prevent nasty ring marks and heat-burns.

French-polished items
Dust regularly with a soft cloth. Remove sticky marks with a cloth wrung out in a warm, mild solution of soapflakes, taking care not to over-wet. Dry thoroughly with a soft cloth. Use a wax polish occasionally and sparingly. Scratches should be dealt with by a professional French polisher.

Lacquered items
Wipe with a damp duster. Apply a fine water-mist spray directly to the duster so that you do not over-wet the wood. Wipe dry and buff with a soft, dry duster. Apply a good furniture polish occasionally to revive the shine. Remove grease and fingermarks with a damp cloth and a mild solution of soapflakes.

Waxed wood
Dust regularly with a soft cloth. Remove sticky marks with a cloth wrung out in a warm, mild solution of soapflakes, taking care not to over-wet. Dry thoroughly with a soft cloth. Apply a wax polish once or twice a year to maintain water-resistance and shine.

HOMEMADE WOOD POLISH
To make your own wood polish, mix two parts olive oil to one part lemon juice. Pour into a pump-spray bottle and use as for normal spray polish. This leaves wood looking lovely and shiny.

tip

Garden furniture

Whether you go for exotic teak or bamboo, hard-wearing metal or practical plastic, your garden furniture needs attention to keep it looking spruce. Here's how to look after your choice of material.

Cane

To remove dust, most items only need vacuuming with an upholstery nozzle or a wipe with a clean, damp cloth. Never leave cane furniture outdoors for long periods of time.

Cast aluminium

Wipe clean with a solution of washing-up liquid. Touch up chipped paint with enamel metal paint after rubbing off any loose bits with wire wool.

Cast and wrought iron

Wearing protective goggles, rub down with wire wool and repaint with anti-rust primer and exterior-grade metal paint. Use a wire brush or rust-removing paint to shift flaking rust. Repaint as for cast aluminium.

Plastic

Wipe clean with a damp cloth and a mild detergent solution. Rinse well. Remove stains with a mild solution of household bleach.

Tubular metal

Wash down plastic-coated tubular metal furniture with a warm solution of washing-up liquid. Protect with a light application of wax polish. Store indoors.

Wood

Durable woods such as teak, oak and mahogany do not usually need preserving. Wipe over with teak oil twice a year to help preserve the colour. Non-durable woods such as ash, elm, beech, redwood, pine and spruce need preserving. Apply a proprietary wood preservative every couple of years.

3

Stains directory

SEVENTY-FIVE INDIVIDUAL STAINS AND HOW TO REMOVE THEM

In this section you will find alphabetical guides to individual stains that are likely to occur throughout the house, in the office and when you're out and about, plus how to cope with life's little accidents.

IN THE KITCHEN AND DINING ROOM

Avocado

A football match on TV, guacamole and tortilla chips, hubby and his greedy friends: a combination that can lead to accidents. The main problem with an avocado stain is that if it is left it will oxidize and eventually turn a nasty grey-black colour. Once this has happened, the stain is almost impossible to remove. Remember, for a good chance of removal, you must act quickly.

General directions Gently scrape the solids off with a blunt knife, taking care not to spread the stain. Follow the directions below for specific fabrics.

Carpet Apply Bissell OxyKIC or White Wizard to the stain. Working from the outside inwards, gently soak up the stain with white paper towels or a clean, white, lint-free cloth. Don't drench the stain – it's better to make repeated small applications than to completely flood the area. Continue until the stain has disappeared. Rinse thoroughly with cold water and blot up as much water as possible with more paper towels. Leave to dry. If any traces remain, a complete carpet shampoo may do the trick.

Washable fabrics After scraping, dampen the mark with cool water and gently rub in a little washing-up liquid. Allow to stand for five minutes or so, then rinse with more cool water. For cotton, follow with a 40°C machine-wash, using biological detergent. For silk, follow with a 30°C machine-wash on the delicates cycle. For wool, follow with a 30°C machine-wash on the delicates cycle.

Dried-on stains Try treating with Dylon Stain Solve before machine-washing as normal.

Banana

One of the baby's favourite foods, but if only she would put it in her mouth, and not all down the front of the white romper suit you have just washed! It may not look like much of a stain when it's fresh, but banana oxidizes to a black colour when it's left. You then have little chance of removing it, so try to deal with it immediately.

General directions Gently scrape off the solids with a blunt knife, taking care not to spread the stain. For older, yellowed stains, try the methods below, but be prepared for limited success. Follow the directions below for specific fabrics.

Carpet Apply Bissell OxyKIC or White Wizard to the stain. Working from the outside inwards, gently soak up the stain with white paper towels or a clean, white, lint-free cloth. Don't drench the stain – it's better to make repeated small applications than to completely flood the area. Continue until the stain has completely disappeared. Rinse thoroughly with cold water and blot up as much water as possible with more paper towels. Leave to dry. If any traces remain, a complete carpet shampoo may be necessary.

Washable fabrics After scraping, dampen the mark and gently rub in a little washing-up liquid. Allow to stand for five minutes, then rinse with plenty of cool water. For cotton, follow with a 40°C machine-wash, using biological detergent. For silk, follow with a 30°C machine-wash on the delicates cycle. For wool, follow with a 30°C machine-wash on the delicates cycle.

Barbecue sauce

Summer. Yes, the dreaded barbecue season, when you´re expected to gratefully receive plate after plate of charred, blackened meat and pretend it tastes good! The only way to get through it is by smothering the lot in barbecue sauce! But that can create problems, too. That gloopy, brown gunk can be hard to remove, especially if you don't deal with it immediately. Act fast or you may just have to accept that the item is ruined – permanently.

General directions Gently blot up as much of the sauce as possible using a blunt knife and white paper towels. Dab at, rather than rub, the stain. Follow the directions below for specific fabrics.

Carpet Spot-treat the affected area with Bissell OxyKIC and, working from the outside inwards, gently soak up the stain, using white paper towels or a clean, white, lint-free cloth. Repeat as necessary until the mark is removed. Be patient. Several applications may be required to get rid of it completely. Finish by blotting with cold water, then allow to dry naturally. If any traces remain, a complete carpet shampoo should do the trick.

All washable fabrics After blotting, rinse the stain under plenty of cold running water until no more colour is removed. For cotton, rub a small amount of liquid detergent into the stain and let it stand for five minutes. Follow with a 40°C machine-wash, using biological detergent. For silk, spot-treat the stained area by blotting thoroughly with a baby wipe tissue and follow with a 30°C machine-wash on the delicates cycle. Allow to dry naturally. Barbecue sauce stains are especially tricky to remove from wool and to have any chance of removing them, you really need to treat the mark within fifteen minutes of it occurring. After rinsing with cold water, cover the affected area with White Wizard and work it gently into the fabric. Use a damp cloth to lift as much of the stain as you can, moving to a clean area of the cloth regularly. Use several applications if necessary. Finish by working a small amount of delicates detergent into the stain, then wash at as high a temperature as the care label permits. Allow to dry naturally. If the stain is not completely removed, try soaking the item in an oxygen-based bleach suitable for wool, following the manufacturer's instructions and checking for colourfastness first.

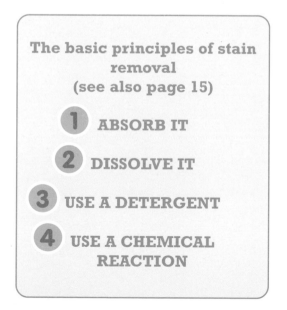

**The basic principles of stain removal
(see also page 15)**

1 **ABSORB IT**

2 **DISSOLVE IT**

3 **USE A DETERGENT**

4 **USE A CHEMICAL REACTION**

Beer

Your hangover might not be so easy to deal with, but the stain's a doddle. Even if you don't notice them until the morning after, beer splashes are fairly easy to remove. Don't leave them for too long though, as the sugar in the beer will caramelize over time, turning the stain a much darker brown and making it more difficult to deal with.

General directions Use white paper towels or a clean, white, lint-free cloth to absorb as much of the stain as possible. Follow the directions below for specific fabrics.

Carpet Apply a proprietary stain remover, such as Bissell OxyKIC, and allow it to work for a few minutes. Blot with more paper towels. Repeat as necessary until the stain has disappeared. Rinse lightly with cold water, and blot as much moisture from the area as possible, again using white paper towels. Leave to dry. For old stains, try dabbing the area with a little methylated spirits.

Washable fabrics After blotting, gently rub in a mild detergent solution (1 tbsp liquid detergent to ½ cup water) mixed with a few drops of distilled white vinegar. Leave to soak for a few minutes. For cotton, follow with a 40°C machine-wash, using biological detergent. For silk and wool, follow with a 30°C machine-wash on the delicates cycle.

Lingering odours For carpets, dampen the affected area and sprinkle generously with bicarbonate of soda. Leave until dry and vacuum up. For fabrics, add a scoop of bicarbonate of soda to the washload.

Beetroot

It tastes sweet and is very good for your health, but beetroot is less good for the well-being of your clothes. However, that cyclamen-pink juice is not as deadly as you might think. Beetroot stains are water-soluble and usually come out quite readily if they have not had time to dry.

General directions Gently scrape away any solid parts with a blunt knife. Use paper towels, or even white bread pressed on the stain, to absorb as much of the juice as possible. Flush with lots of cool water. Follow the directions below for specific fabrics.

Carpet Treat the stain with Bissell OxyKIC, following the manufacturer's instructions. You will probably find you need to make repeated applications, but keep going – the stain should come out eventually.

Washable fabrics Scrape, blot and flush with water as above. For cotton, follow with a 40°C machine-wash, using biological detergent. For silk, follow with a 30°C machine-wash on the delicates cycle. For wool, treat with Stain Devils No. 6 and follow with a 30°C machine-wash on the delicates cycle.

tip

JUICY BEETROOT
When preparing beetroot, avoid staining your hands by wearing disposable latex gloves. Peel beetroot after, rather than before, cooking to help limit the leaching of their juices. If you end up with stained hands or chopping boards, the marks will come off if rubbed with lemon juice.

Blackcurrants and other berries

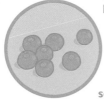

Berries are undoubtedly delicious, but they can also be messy. Don't worry though – that lurid splatter down the front of your favourite shirt looks worse than it is. Blackcurrants and other berries leave pigment-based stains, which are soluble in water and usually easy to remove if you act quickly.

General directions Blot up as much of the stain as possible with white paper towels or a clean, white, lint-free cloth. Dab, rather than rub, at the stain. Follow the directions below for specific fabrics.

Carpet Cover the stain with White Wizard and, working from the outside inwards, gently soak up the stain, again using white paper towels or a clean, white, lint-free cloth. Don't be tempted to drench the area – it's better to make repeated small applications. Continue until the stain has completely disappeared. If traces still remain, a complete carpet shampoo may be necessary.

Washable fabrics After blotting, rinse the stain under plenty of cold running water. For cotton, follow immediately with a 40°C machine-wash, using biological detergent. For silk, treat with Stain Devils No. 6 and follow with a 30°C machine-wash on the delicates cycle. Berry stains are tricky to remove from wool and the key is to act immediately. After rinsing with cold water, spray lightly with Wine Away until the stain turns blue. Blot again, and repeat this process until the stain has completely disappeared. Then wash at as high a temperature as the care label permits.

Burnt pans

So engrossed in reading the latest salacious showbiz gossip that you forgot about the stew bubbling away on the stove? Now it's a charred, blackened mess burned onto the base of your best saucepan! Forget about cooking dinner, order a take-away instead, and get to work restoring your prized pan. You'll have it back in tip-top condition before the food's even arrived.

What to do Fill the pan with water and throw in a dishwasher tablet or 1 tbsp biological washing powder. Place it on the hob and bring to the boil. Leave to simmer for around ten minutes. All those nasty burnt bits will simply lift away, leaving your pan as good as new. Repeat as necessary, then wash thoroughly as normal. You can also use this method for hob-safe roasting tins.

Always refer to the Golden Rules of Stain Removal on pages 14–19

tip

BEAT THE BURN
For cooking scrambled eggs or other foods that tend to stick, invest in a good-quality, hard-anodized saucepan. These are so easy to clean, it's laughable, even when burnt. Simply wipe with a sponge and the mess will usually come right off.

Carrot

Stains from orange vegetables, such as carrots, pumpkins and sweet potatoes, are caused by the pigment beta-carotene. Beta-carotene is good for your night vision, but not for your clothes, on which the stains it deposits can be a real pain. Here's what to do.

General directions Gently scrape up any solids with a blunt knife. Blot the area with white paper towels. Follow the directions below for specific fabrics.

Carpet Treat the stain with Bissell OxyKIC, following the manufacturer's instructions. You will probably need to make repeated applications, but the stain should come out eventually.

Washable fabrics Flush the affected area with cool water to remove as much of the stain as possible. Blot with white paper towels. For cotton, follow with a 40°C machine-wash, using biological detergent. For silk, follow with a 30°C machine-wash on the delicates cycle. Wool is tricky. If you act fast, washing at 30°C may work, but if the stain has dried, it probably won't come out. Finally, try repeated applications of Dylon Stain Solve.

tip

DON'T GO ORANGE
If puréeing carrots leaves your food processor bowl covered with an orange-coloured film, try wiping vegetable oil around the bowl, then washing as normal. Doing this will often remove the marks.

Chewing gum

In Singapore you can actually be fined for chewing gum in a public place. Not because they particularly have anything against it, but because people spit and stick their chewed-up gum all over pavements and other surfaces. Then some poor, unsuspecting soul inadvertently sits on it! Not only is this disgusting, it can also be one of the messiest stains to remove.

General directions If possible, put the entire item in the freezer and leave until the gum is brittle enough to be picked off with a blunt knife. Otherwise, place an ice pack or bag of frozen peas over the gum until it hardens, then pick off as much as possible. Follow the directions below for specific fabrics.

Carpet Use White Wizard or WD-40 to remove any remaining traces. Lightly cover the affected area, leave to work for a minute, then blot with paper towels to lift the gum. Rinse by blotting with damp paper towels.

Washable fabrics For cotton, machine-wash at 40°C using biological detergent. For silk, spot-treat the area with Stain Devils No. 3, following the manufacturer's instructions, then machine-wash at 30°C on the delicates cycle. For wool, spot-treat with Sticky Stuff Remover, following the manufacturer's instructions, then machine-wash at 30°C on the delicates cycle.

Chewing gum in hair There is no solution that is one hundred per cent effective, but rubbing peanut butter or vegetable oil into the gum will help to soften it and make it easier to remove.

Chocolate

Your true love follows tradition and buys you chocolates for Valentine's Day, despite the fact that you have told him you're dieting and would prefer something non-edible... like diamonds, say. Nevertheless, you ate them anyway and now have greasy brown smears around your mouth, your clothes and on everything else within ten metres! Clean up now or the evidence will be permanent.

General directions Blot or gently scrape up deposits, using a blunt knife and white paper towels. Follow the directions below for specific fabrics.

Carpet Spot-treat the affected area with Bissell OxyKIC and gently soak up the stain with white paper towels. Repeat as necessary, and finish by lightly rinsing with water and blotting again to remove as much moisture as possible.

Washable fabrics For cotton, steep the item in a biological pre-soaking agent, such as Biotex or Biz, for fifteen to thirty minutes. Gently rub the affected area every five minutes or so. Follow by machine-washing at 40°C with biological detergent. For silk and wool, pre-soak as for cotton, but in a solution of washing soda crystals and water. Follow by machine-washing at 30°C on the delicates cycle.

tip

STICKY CHOCOLATE
Chocolate has a very low melting point, so putting it in the fridge to firm up before eating will help avoid sticky fingers and consequent stains.

Cloudy glasses

This is a very common household problem and is usually caused by the repeated washing of glassware in a dishwasher. Over time, the energetic action of the machine etches the glass with tiny scratches, in which limescale may build up. The combination of these two

things causes the characteristic cloudiness. Unfortunately, if you've left it too long and the etching is very bad, the damage will be permanent. Try the remedies below.

What to do Fill the dishwasher's detergent dispenser with citric acid crystals (available from pharmacies and hardware stores) and run the glasses through a normal wash, without using any detergent. The citric acid acts as a limescale remover, and will also descale the dishwasher at the same time. If this doesn't work, try soaking the glasses overnight in neat white vinegar, then rinse in cold water.

tip

SPARKLING GLASSWARE
You should always wash glassware by hand. Use warm water and washing-up liquid, then rinse in clean water. Dry with a soft linen cloth. If you must use the dishwasher, make sure it is always topped up with adequate salt and rinse aid, and remove glasses before the drying cycle starts – high temperatures accelerate the etching process. Alternatively, buy cheap glassware that you won't mind replacing every couple of years!

Coffee with milk

Over-enthusiasm for that first hit of caffeine during the rush to work can lead to accidents, and unless you act fast, you're likely to be left with a permanent reminder – coffee stains can be hard to shift. This is because the proteins in milk are affected by heat and are liable to coagulate and set into fabrics such as wool, even at low temperatures (see Pigment- and Tannin-based Stains, page 23).

General directions Gently blot up as much of the stain as possible with white paper towels or a clean, white, lint-free cloth. Dab, rather than rub, at the stain. Follow the directions below for specific fabrics.

Carpet Cover the stain with White Wizard and, working from the outside inwards, gently soak up the stain with white paper towels or a clean, white, lint-free cloth. Make repeated small applications rather than completely drenching the area. Continue until the stain has completely disappeared.

Washable fabrics After blotting, rinse the stain under plenty of cold running water. For cotton, follow immediately with a 40°C machine-wash, using biological detergent. For silk, treat with Stain Devils No. 2 or No. 4 and follow with a 30°C machine-wash on the delicates cycle. If the item is wool, you'll need to act fast to prevent it being ruined. After rinsing with cold water, soak in a cool solution of washing soda crystals or a suitable pre-wash detergent. Then hand-wash in lukewarm water and leave to dry naturally. If this doesn't work, re-wet the item and rub a little glycerine into the stain, then leave it to stand for approximately thirty minutes before hand-washing again as above.

Cola and other fizzy drinks

A shaken-up bottle of fizzy drink can leave an alarming spray of colour over your clothing, but it's not hard to wash out. The main thing you need to know is that the sugar in these fizzy drinks will oxidize and cause the stain to darken over a period of time, making it more difficult to remove. So, as with all stains, the best thing to do is act immediately.

General directions Gently blot up as much of the stain as possible with white paper towels or a clean, white, lint-free cloth. Dab, rather than rub, at the stain. Follow the directions below for specific fabrics.

Carpet Cover the stain with Bissell OxyKIC and, working from the outside inwards, gently blot the stain with white paper towels or a clean, white, lint-free cloth. Make repeated small applications rather than completely soaking the area. Continue until the stain has completely disappeared.

Washable fabrics After blotting, rinse the stain under plenty of cold running water. For cotton, follow with a 40°C machine-wash, using biological detergent. For silk, follow with a 30°C machine-wash on the delicates cycle. For wool, follow with a 30°C machine-wash on the delicates cycle.

Always refer to the Golden Rules of Stain Removal on pages 14–19

Curry

Stains from curry are usually caused by the pigment curcumin, which is found in turmeric. It is one of the toughest stains known to man, and the best advice here is not to eat curry while wearing silk or wool. There's no foolproof way to get rid of a turmeric stain, but if you act quickly enough, the following suggestions might just do the trick.

General directions Use white paper towels to absorb as much of the stain as you can. Apply methylated spirits to the stained area and leave it for a short time. The mark will turn bright red initially, but don't be alarmed – this is quite normal. Blot with white paper towels to remove as much colour as possible, moving to a clean area of the towel regularly. Repeat this process until there is no further transfer of colour to the towels. Flush with cold water, then apply a mild detergent solution to the stained area. Allow this to soak in for a few minutes, then machine-wash the item as normal, at as high a temperature as the fabric allows. If traces still remain, you'll be pleased to hear that curcumin is unstable when exposed to light, and placing the affected item in direct sun for a few days will fade the stain further.

Carpet White Wizard is the proprietary product that is most effective for removing curry stains.

Worktops and other surfaces A slightly abrasive paste made from bicarbonate of soda and water works well on curry stains on hard surfaces.

Always refer to the Golden Rules of Stain Removal on pages 14–19

Cutlery stains

Stains frequently appear on cutlery. Hot grease may leave a stubborn, rainbow-coloured mark, and mineral salts in tap water can cause a white film if the cutlery is not dried thoroughly. Acidic foods such as vinegar may also cause staining, while the humid atmosphere inside a dishwasher may pit the surface of stainless steel and cause 'rust' marks (see **Kitchenware, page 88**).

General directions A proprietary stainless-steel cleaner will remove most marks, or rub with a cloth soaked in vinegar or lemon juice, then rinse thoroughly.

Knives Stainless-steel knives are more prone to corroding than stainless-steel forks or spoons. This is because in order to achieve a lasting, sharp edge, the steel used in the knife blade must be much harder than that used for other cutlery. This results in it having reduced resistance to corroding. To keep your chopping knives in tip-top condition, don't leave them immersed in water for long periods and always hand wash, then dry them thoroughly with a tea towel.

Tea-stained teaspoons Soak overnight in a cupful of water mixed with biological washing detergent. Rinse and wash thoroughly after soaking.

tip

DISHWASHING
Never use the rinse and hold cycle on the dishwasher for cutlery, and always remove stainless-steel cutlery as soon as the normal dishwashing cycle has ended.

Egg

Runny yolk dripping off toast soldiers is one way that eggy stains can find their way on to your shirt. Egg is a protein-based stain and needs to be treated at a low temperature so that it doesn't coagulate and set into the fabric. It's usually quite easy to remove.

General directions Gently scrape off any solid bits with a blunt knife, then blot up as much liquid as possible with white paper towels. Follow the directions below for specific fabrics.

Carpet Spot-treat with a proprietary carpet shampoo, then rinse with cold water and blot dry.

Washable fabrics After blotting, flush the affected area with lots of cold water. For cotton, follow by machine-washing at 40°C with biological detergent. If the stains are old, soak overnight in a solution of an enzyme-based stain remover and cold water. Machine-wash as normal. For silk and wool, rub a little mild detergent solution into the affected area, then wash at 30°C on the delicates cycle.

Fats, grease and oils

Not as bad as you might think. The butter that dripped from your toast or the oil that spattered you from the frying pan will come out if you act quickly and use the right approach. The main thing to remember is not to sponge with cold water, as this can set the stain.

General directions Sprinkle unscented talcum powder or cornflour over the stain to cover it. Leave for five minutes, then remove with a soft brush. If obvious signs of grease remain, try using white paper towels to absorb more of it. Follow the directions below for specific fabrics.

Carpet Treat the affected area with White Wizard, then blot with lightly dampened white paper towels. Leave to dry.

Washable fabrics For cotton, rub a little washing-up liquid into the stain, then machine-wash immediately at 40°C with biological detergent. For silk and wool, spot-treat with Stain Devils No. 5, following the manufacturer's instructions. Then machine-wash at as high a temperature as the garment allows, using a detergent for delicates.

Gravy

 We all love Sunday lunch with all the trimmings, but those trimmings can be a nightmare for our clothes. Gravy is a combination stain, which contains mainly protein and grease. You need to deal with the greasy part of the stain first, and then use a low wash temperature so that the protein part does not coagulate and set into the fabric. As always, for best results you need to act fast.

General directions Gently scrape off as much residue as possible with a blunt knife. Apply a few drops of methylated spirits to the stain and blot with white paper towels or a clean, white, lint-free cloth until no more of the stain appears to be transferring to the towels. Allow the solvent to evaporate completely. Follow the directions below for specific fabrics.

Carpet Apply White Wizard to the affected area and blot gently with a dampened paper towel until the stain has been removed. Leave to dry.

Washable fabrics For cotton, after blotting with methylated spirits, put the item in a 40°C machine-wash with biological detergent. If the stain is large, work a few drops of liquid detergent into it before washing. For stubborn stains, try soaking the item in an enzyme-based pre-soaking agent before washing as normal. It can be tricky to remove gravy from silk. After blotting, rub a little detergent for delicates directly on the stain before machine-washing at 30°C on the delicates cycle. If the stain remains, take the item to a dry-cleaner, who may be able to remove it. For wool, after blotting, spot-treat the stained area with Stain Devils No. 5 (following the manufacturer's instructions), then wash at 30°C on the delicates cycle.

Ice cream

We can't eat ice creams quickly enough when the summer sun is beating down, determined to make them melt straight on to our clothing. Ice cream is another combination stain. Most flavours contain grease, protein and pigment but despite this, ice cream is usually fairly easy to remove. Don't use a high wash temperature or you may set the protein part of the stain into the fabric.

General directions Gently scrape off as much ice cream as possible with a blunt knife, then blot with white paper towels. Follow the directions below for specific fabrics.

Carpet Spot-treat the affected area with a proprietary carpet shampoo such as Bissell OxyKIC. Rinse with cool water, and blot to dry.

Washable fabrics Rub a small amount of liquid detergent into the affected area, and leave to soak for a few minutes. For cotton, machine-wash at 40°C with biological detergent. For silk and wool, machine-wash at 30°C on the delicates cycle.

tip

FLAVOURED ICE CREAM
Some ice creams, such as chocolate or raspberry flavour, tend to be more highly coloured. If the removal methods described here don't completely remove the stain, try the techniques described for the individual foods. See chocolate on page 108 and raspberry juice on page 126.

Jam

Jam and jelly stains are sugar- and pigment-based, so will usually be soluble in water. Some types are likely to contain tannins, so never use salt. Pigment stains are difficult to remove once they have had time to dry on fabric. You need to act immediately.

General directions Gently scrape off as much residue as you can with a blunt knife. Follow the directions below for specific fabrics.

Carpet Use Bissell OxyKIC or White Wizard to spot-treat the affected area. Blot the stain with white paper towels or a clean, white, lint-free cloth. Rinse with cool water. Blot dry with white paper towels.

Washable fabrics Gently rub White Wizard into the affected area and leave for a few minutes. Blot up as much colour as you can with white paper towels. Flush the stain with lots of cool water. For cotton, machine-wash at 40°C with biological detergent. For silk and wool, machine-wash at 30°C on the delicates cycle.

tip

JUICY FRUITS
If the removal methods described here don't completely remove the stain, try the techniques described for individual fruits, such as blackcurrants (page 104), peach juice (page 124), raspberry juice (page 126).

Mango

Mangoes are one of the messiest fruits to eat, which is risky because the stain from their juice is lethal. It is virtually impossible to remove from wool, and you'll need perseverance to remove it from other fabrics. The best way to eat mangoes is while leaning over a sink to catch the drips!

General directions Gently scrape off any solid residue with a blunt knife. Follow the directions below for specific fabrics.

Carpet Use white paper towels to blot as much liquid as possible from the stain. Spot-treat with Bissell OxyKIC, following the manufacturer's instructions. You may need to make repeated applications, so have patience.

Washable fabrics Flush the affected area with lots of cool water. Rub a little White Wizard into the stain and leave for five minutes. Blot with dry paper towels to lift as much colour as possible. For cotton, follow by machine-washing at 40°C with a biological detergent. For silk and wool, follow by machine-washing at as hot a temperature as the fabric allows, using a detergent for delicates.

Other things to try If the stain still remains after the above treatment, try soaking the item in an oxygen-based, colour-safe bleaching product (see Tools for the Job, page 26). Always check the fabric care label first and test for colourfastness.

> **Always refer to the Golden Rules of Stain Removal on pages 14–19**

Mayonnaise

Mayonnaise always seems to squirt out of the sides of sandwiches, no matter how delicately you bite into them. It makes a stain similar to grease and usually washes out very easily without any special treatment.

General directions Lift as much solid residue as possible with a blunt knife. Try not to spread the stain. Follow the directions below for specific fabrics.

Carpet White Wizard, applied to the affected area, works well. Cover the stain and blot with dry paper towels until all traces are removed. Blot with a damp cloth to rinse and allow to dry.

Washable fabrics Rub a little White Wizard or liquid detergent into the affected area. For cotton, follow by machine-washing at 40°C with biological detergent. For silk and wool, follow by machine-washing at 30°C on the delicates cycle. If the stain has dried before washing, try applying a few drops of methylated spirits to the affected area and blotting with a white paper towel. Allow the solvent to evaporate, then rub a small amount of liquid detergent into the area before washing as normal.

Milk and cream

As the saying goes, it's no use crying over spilt milk. Nor do you need to, because milk and cream come out of most fabrics quite easily. This is mainly a protein stain (although cream also contains a certain amount of fat), so the water you use needs to be at a low temperature.

General directions Blot as much liquid from the stain as you can with white paper towels or a clean, white, lint-free cloth. Flush with lots of cool water. Follow the directions below for specific fabrics.

Carpet Spot-treat the affected area with a proprietary carpet cleaner, such as Bissell OxyKIC; you can also use White Wizard. Follow the manufacturer's instructions. Rinse with cool water and use paper towels to blot dry – it's very important to lift as much moisture as possible, otherwise you may be left with a foul sour milk stench coming from the carpet. For lingering 'sour milk' odours, sprinkle bicarbonate of soda over the area and leave for a few hours before vacuuming. If that doesn't work, a specialized product designed for removing pet smells should do the trick.

Washable fabrics Rub a small amount of liquid clothes detergent into the stained area and leave for a few minutes. For cotton, follow by machine-washing at 40°C with biological detergent. For silk and wool, follow by machine-washing at 30°C on the delicates cycle.

> **Milk and cream come out of most fabrics quite easily**

Mustard

A must on burgers and hot dogs, but not on your clothes. Unfortunately, once there, it's very difficult to remove. The colouring in mustard usually comes from turmeric, the culprit responsible for those fiendish yellow curry stains (see Curry, page 112).

General directions Gently scrape off any solid residue with a blunt knife. Dampen the affected area with a few drops of methylated spirits. The stain may turn dark red, but don't worry, this is normal. Blot up as much colour as you can with white paper towels. To avoid spreading the stain, use a delicate dabbing motion, and work from the outside inwards. Follow the directions below for specific fabrics.

Carpet Bissell OxyKIC and White Wizard are most effective on mustard stains. After blotting, apply either product to the stained area, following the manufacturer's instructions. Rinse as directed. Allow to dry naturally.

Washable fabrics Allow the methylated spirits to evaporate completely. Then spray the affected area on both sides with De.Solv.It. Leave for five minutes before blotting with a clean white cloth. Reapply De.Solv.It and then wash the item according to fabric type. For cotton, follow by machine-washing at 40°C with biological detergent. For silk and wool, follow by machine-washing at 30°C on the delicates cycle.

If the marks persist Try soaking the item in a colour-safe, oxygen-based bleaching product, but check the care label first. If all else fails, hang the item out in the sun for a few days. The pigment in mustard is unstable in light, so exposure to the sun will help to fade it.

Orange juice

A breakfast favourite, packed with healthy vitamin C – orange juice is not usually a problem if you spill it down your white work shirt. Although it is a pigment-based stain, it is soluble in water and should come out quite readily if you deal with it quickly.

General directions Blot up as much liquid as you can with white paper towels. Follow the directions below for specific fabrics.

Carpet Apply any proprietary carpet stain treatment, following the manufacturer's instructions. Leave to dry.

Washable fabrics After blotting, flush the affected area with cool water. For cotton, follow by machine-washing at 40°C with biological detergent. For silk and wool, follow by machine-washing at 30°C on the delicates cycle.

Stains on your juicer If the plastic bowl has become stained orange, try wiping vegetable oil around the bowl, then wash as normal. Alternatively, make a paste of two parts bicarbonate of soda and one part water and use the paste to scrub around the inside of the bowl. Leave to stand for thirty minutes or so, then wash as normal using a nylon scrubber and rinse in clear water. To help prevent stains re-occurring, always rinse the bowl (and any other stainable parts) with cool water as soon as you have finished using it.

Peach juice

Biting into a perfectly ripe, fresh peach is one of life's pleasures, but you should always have a napkin to hand to catch the drips. The pigment in the juice is a powerful staining agent and hard to remove unless it's dealt with immediately. However, it is water-based and if you act quickly, you should be able to get it out. Here's what to do.

General directions Gently blot up as much of the stain as possible using white paper towels or a clean, white, lint-free cloth. Dab, rather than rub, at the stain. Follow the directions below for specific fabrics.

Carpet Cover the stain with Bissell OxyKIC and, working from the outside inwards, gently soak up the mark with white paper towels or a clean, white, lint-free cloth. Don't drench the area – it's better to use repeated small applications. Continue until the stain has disappeared, then blot with cold water and allow to dry naturally. Follow with a complete carpet shampoo if necessary.

Washable fabrics After blotting, rinse the stain under plenty of cold running water until no more colour is removed. Work a small amount of liquid detergent into any remaining stained area and leave to stand for five minutes or so. For cotton, immediately follow with a 40°C machine-wash, using biological detergent. For silk and wool, follow with a 30°C machine-wash on the delicates cycle. Allow the item to dry naturally. If any traces of the stain remain, try soaking the item in an oxygen-based bleach. Follow the manufacturer's instructions and always test for colourfastness first.

Pomegranate juice

It's reputedly a super-food bar none, packed with antioxidants and possibly providing all sorts of nutritional benefits. Unfortunately, that ruby-red juice is also a super stainer. Unless you've spilt it on cotton that can be washed at a high temperature, be prepared for disappointment – it's almost impossible to remove.

General directions Your best chance of success is to try immersing the affected item in a biological pre-soaking agent before washing. (This is one instance where you can forget the advice about not using this type of product on silk and wool. The item will be ruined by the stain if you do nothing, so what have you got to lose?) If that doesn't work, soaking in a colour-safe, oxygen-based bleaching product may shift the stain. Don't hold out too much hope though – there's a reason why pomegranate juice has been used for centuries as a natural fabric dye!

Always refer to the Golden Rules of Stain Removal on pages 14–19

Raspberry juice

Blowing raspberries is much more fun than getting them on your clothes! The day-glo pink juice is almost impossible to remove once it dries, and can leave a permanent reminder of your accident. However, raspberry juice is a water-based stain and if you deal with it while it is still fresh (within fifteen minutes or so of the stain occurring), you may be in with a chance. Act fast!

General directions Gently blot up as much of the stain as possible with white paper towels or a clean, white, lint-free cloth. Dab, rather than rub, the stain. Follow the directions below for specific fabrics.

Carpet Spot-treat the stain with Bissell OxyKIC, following the manufacturer's instructions. Use white paper towels or a clean, white, lint-free cloth to absorb the mark. Continue until the stain has disappeared. If traces still remain, a complete carpet shampoo may be necessary.

Washable fabrics After blotting, rinse the stain under cold running water until no further colour is removed. For cotton, rub a small amount of liquid detergent into the stain, preferably one that contains enzymes. Leave for five minutes. Immediately follow with a 40°C machine-wash, using biological detergent. For wool and silk, act immediately. After rinsing with cold water, spot-treat the area with any 'oxi-action' type product suitable for use on wool and silk. Follow the manufacturer's instructions, then wash at as high a temperature as the care label permits.

Persistent stains If the stain remains, soak the item in a solution of oxygen-based bleach and water. Follow the manufacturer's instructions and test for colourfastness first.

Red wine

There are lots of myths surrounding the removal of red wine stains. The most common is the one about sprinkling salt on the stain – **DON'T DO IT!** Red wine stains contain tannin and can be set permanently by the application of salt.

First aid If the stain has occurred while you're out at dinner, and you can't treat it immediately, flush the affected area with sparkling water – the bubbles in the water will help push the stain out of the fabric. Then, when you get home, you can treat the mark properly with a miraculous product called Wine Away.

General directions Blot up as much moisture as you can with white paper towels or a clean, white, lint-free cloth. Follow the directions below for specific fabrics.

Carpet Spray the affected area with Wine Away and leave for a few minutes. Blot with white paper towels to lift the stain. Repeat as necessary.

Washable fabrics Flush the stained area with cool water. Apply Wine Away and leave for a few minutes. The stain will turn blue first, then start disappearing. Blot to remove the remaining colour and repeat if necessary. Then machine-wash according to fabric type. For cotton, wash at 40°C with biological detergent. For silk and wool, wash at 30°C on the delicates cycle.

WARNING

Never sprinkle salt on a red wine stain.

Soy sauce

It may be the cornerstone of Asian cuisine, but when it gets spilt on clothes, the dark brown stain looks frightening. Don't worry – it's basically a pigment stain (particularly the cheaper brands, which often add caramel colouring to darken the sauce) and comes out easily as long as you deal with it quickly.

General directions Use white paper towels to blot as much liquid as you can from the stain. Follow the directions below for specific fabrics.

Carpet Apply White Wizard to the stain. Allow to stand for a few minutes, then blot with lightly dampened, white paper towels or a clean, white, lint-free cloth. Rinse to remove any remaining traces. Allow the carpet to dry.

Washable fabrics Flush the stained area with lots of cool water. This alone should get rid of most of it. Then gently rub White Wizard into any remaining stain and leave to stand for a few minutes. Blot with paper towels, then machine-wash according to fabric type. For cotton, wash at 40°C with biological detergent. For silk and wool, wash at 30°C on the delicates cycle.

Tea

Spilt your morning cuppa? Like coffee, tea is a tannin-based stain (see Pigment- and Tannin-based stains, page 23). Don't sprinkle salt on it as this can set it, and act fast (especially if the spill is on silk or wool) or the mark will be difficult to remove. If the tea has milk in it, don't use a high wash temperature as this may set the protein in the milk.

General directions Gently blot up as much of the stain as possible with white paper towels or a clean, white, lint-free cloth. Dab, rather than rub, at the stain. Follow the directions below for specific fabrics.

Carpet Cover the stain with White Wizard and, working from the outside inwards, dab with white paper towels or a clean, white, lint-free cloth to soak up the stain. Make repeated small applications rather than completely flooding the area. Continue until the stain has disappeared.

Washable fabrics After blotting, rinse the stain under plenty of cold running water. For cotton, follow immediately with a 40°C machine-wash, using biological detergent. For silk, treat with Stain Devils No. 2 or No. 4 and follow with a 30°C machine-wash on the delicates cycle. With wool, you'll need to tackle the stain quickly to prevent the item being ruined. After rinsing with cold water, soak in a cool solution of washing soda crystals or a suitable pre-wash detergent. Then hand-wash in lukewarm water and leave to dry naturally. If this doesn't work, re-wet the item and rub a little glycerine into the stain, then leave for about thirty minutes before hand-washing again as above.

Tomato-based soups and sauces

Bolognese, ketchup, soup... Mama mia! Tomato-based food stains are one of the worst to remove. They are complex products that contain proteins, fats and highly coloured pigments. If you don't attack this type of stain immediately, you can forget it! The only way you'll get the stain out is with scissors. However, if you get on the case straight away, you might just be in with a chance.

General directions Place an absorbent pad under the stain. Gently scrape off any solid parts with a blunt knife. Blot the stain with white paper towels to remove as much as possible. Apply a few drops of solvent, such as methylated spirits, and blot again, moving frequently to clean areas of the absorbent pad and changing the area of the paper towel as soon as it has colour on it. Repeat until no more of the stain is lifted with the towels. Let the solvent evaporate completely. If you are tackling a dry stain on the carpet or on washable fabric, soften it first by working in a solution of equal parts glycerine and water.

Leave to stand for a few minutes, then rinse and follow the methods above according to fabric type.

Carpet After treating with solvent, cover the affected area with White Wizard and leave to work for a few minutes. Blot with white paper towels, then rinse with cool water and blot dry. If traces of the stain still remain, you may need to have the entire carpet cleaned professionally.

Plastic food containers and food processor bowls First try wiping all over the stained area with vegetable oil before washing as normal – if the stain is fresh, the oil will often lift out the colour. If this doesn't work, make a paste of two parts bicarbonate of soda and one part water and apply the paste to the stain. Rub in well with a nylon scrubber, then wash in soapy water and rinse as normal.

Washable fabrics After treating with solvent, apply a few drops of mild detergent solution and work it into the stain. Leave for five minutes, then flush with lots of cool water. Follow by applying Stain Devils No. 5, according to the manufacturer's instructions. Finally, machine-wash according to fabric type. For cotton, wash at 40°C with biological detergent (you could also soak the item in an enzyme-based pre-soaking agent before washing). For silk and wool,

wash at 30°C on the delicates cycle. As a last resort, soak the item in a colour-safe, oxygen-based bleaching product to remove any last traces of the stain. Check the fabric care label and test for colourfastness on an inconspicuous area first.

Always refer to the Golden Rules of Stain Removal on pages 14–19

tip

KEEP PLASTIC FANTASTIC
Prevent tomato-based foods from staining plastic tubs and bowls by lightly coating the container with oil spray before adding the food. It's also a good idea to allow the food to cool to room temperature before storing it in plastic – heat contributes to the staining process.

BATHROOM AND BEAUTY

Antiperspirant deodorant

In your rush to leave the house, you didn't let your antiperspirant dry before getting dressed and now have unpleasant white marks on your clothes. Don't confuse fresh antiperspirant stains with the nastier, yellowy stains caused by perspiration – those build up over time and are much more difficult to remove. Marks left by antiperspirant normally wash out quite readily if dealt with quickly.

Instant remedy If you are wearing a sleeveless top and the dreaded marks have appeared, a quick swab with a baby wipe tissue will get rid of them.

General directions Before washing the garment, the one thing you need to do is to rinse the affected area under cool water.

This will prevent chemicals in the antiperspirant being 'fixed' by hot water in the washing machine and causing a permanent stain. Incidentally, doing this to the underarm area of all clothing before washing it will also help to stop long-term perspiration stains from developing. Launder the garment according to fabric type.

tip

STREAKY DEODORANT
To avoid embarrassing streaks, always let your antiperspirant dry completely before you get dressed, particularly the gel and roll-on types. Don't use more product than necessary, it doesn't make it work better and will simply result in more being transferred to your clothes.

Fake tan

If you want to avoid fake tan stains completely, you'll just have to accept that being 'pale and interesting' is the only way to go. Depending on the brand and the length of time it has had to develop, fake tan can be impossible to remove, and many a bride has lived to regret applying that last-minute 'instant glow', which then transferred itself permanently to her wedding dress! If you're lucky and the brand is one of the less tenacious types, try the following remedies.

General directions Proprietary fake tan removers are available and although these are designed to remove product from the skin, it's worth trying them out on stained garments too, if all else fails. Just be careful before applying to check for colour-fastness on an inconspicuous area first. Follow the directions for specific fabrics.

Washable fabrics Often, a 40°C wash with biological detergent will get rid of marks on sheets and cotton clothing. For silk and wool, rub with a warm solution of washing-up liquid, followed by a 30°C wash.

tip

APPLYING FAKE TAN

To avoid staining your clothes, always apply fake tan a few hours before you get dressed so it has time to dry. Wash your hands afterwards so you don't end up with brown 'nicotine-like' nails! For more even colour when applying fake tan, exfoliate your skin first.

Foundation

So you thought you'd been a good girl and carefully removed all traces of your 'face' before bedtime, despite being tired and tipsy after several glasses of wine! Instead, you've woken up to find brown smears all over your pillowcases. Surprisingly, foundation does usually come out of most materials. As always, deal with the stain as soon as possible and have the right removal product to hand.

General directions Gently scrape off any solid residue with a blunt knife. Follow the directions below for specific fabrics.

Carpet Apply White Wizard to the affected area. Leave it to work for a few minutes, then use white paper towels to soak up the stain. Work from the outside inwards to avoid spreading the stain. Repeat as necessary. Finish by dabbing the area with a dampened paper towel to rinse it, then blot dry.

Washable fabrics For cotton, spray the affected area lightly with De.Solv.It, then follow the manufacturer's instructions. Repeat as necessary, then machine-wash on as high a temperature as the fabric allows, using biological detergent. If the stain persists, try immersing in a biological pre-soaking agent before rewashing. For silk and wool, spot-treat the stained area with Stain Devils No. 5, according to the manufacturer's instructions. Wash at 30°C on the delicates cycle.

> **Always refer to the Golden Rules of Stain Removal on pages 14–19**

Lipstick

It's a tricky one, but with patience it can be removed. Lipstick is a complex stain containing both grease and highly coloured pigments. You need to dissolve the greasy part first and then deal with the dye. So, if your sultry new lipstick has managed to transfer itself to your clothes, here's how to fix the problem.

General directions Very gently, scrape off any lumpy bits with a blunt knife, being careful not to spread the stain.

Carpet Squirt a few drops of WD-40 on the affected area, wait thirty seconds, then blot with white paper towels, moving to clean areas of the towel frequently. Work from the outside inwards, and use a delicate dabbing motion. You must be gentle to avoid pushing the stain deeper into the carpet or spreading it. Repeat until no more of the stain is lifted. Remove remaining traces of colour with White Wizard. Apply to the mark and leave for a minute or so, then blot with lightly dampened paper towels or a clean, white, lint-free cloth. Dab the area with clean water to rinse, then blot dry. Repeat until stain is removed.

Washable fabrics On cotton, if the stain is small, it will often come out if you rub in a little liquid detergent and wash as normal. For larger or deep-coloured stains, pre-treat with De.Solv.It according to manufacturer's instructions and then machine-wash at 40°C with biological detergent. For silk, use the WD-40 method as described for carpet, followed by Stain Devils No. 3 to remove the greasy mark that WD-40 may leave. Then machine-wash at 30°C on the delicates cycle. For wool, spot-treat with De.Solv.It, then wash at 30°C on the delicates cycle.

Mascara

Waterproof mascara might be brilliant in the rain, or when you want to have a little cry without ruining your make-up, but unfortunately, no matter how carefully you take it off at night, it always seems to leave traces all over the pillowcase and sheets the following morning. You should be able to remove it without too much trouble if you act quickly enough.

General directions Carefully scrape up any solids with a blunt knife or white paper towels. Follow the directions below for specific fabrics.

Carpet Spot-treat the affected area with Bissell OxyKIC, according to the manufacturer's instructions. Repeat as necessary until the stain has been removed. Rinse with cool water and blot with paper towels to dry.

Washable fabrics Spot-treat with Stain Devils No. 3, following the manufacturer's instructions, then wash at as high a temperature as the fabric permits. Allow to dry naturally.

tip

REMOVING MASCARA
If you've run out of eye make-up remover, wiping your lashes with baby oil on cotton wool will often remove mascara very effectively and stop it escaping onto your pillow at night.

Nail polish

If the nail polish has dried, you can forget it – nail polish is virtually impossible to get out with any home treatment. Take the item to a dry-cleaner, who might be able to help. If the spill is tiny though, and you act instantly, you may be in with a chance. Good luck!

General directions Immediately dab the area with a cotton bud that has been very slightly dampened with nail polish remover, but do not use on acetate fabric. Repeat until no more colour comes off. Follow the directions below for specific fabrics.

Carpet If traces remain, you may be able to remove them by snipping off the tips of the carpet tufts in the affected area with scissors.

Washable fabrics Next, launder according to fabric type. Any remaining stain may be removable by bleaching. Check the care label first and test for colourfastness.

Stains on hard surfaces Moisten a white paper towel with nail polish remover and gently dab over the stain until it is removed. Wipe over with a clean damp cloth and polish dry. Be careful on varnished surfaces as the polish remover may damage the finish – test on an inconspicuous area first.

WARNING

CAUTION
Do not use nail polish remover on acetate fabric.

Perfume

This is a sneaky one. Perfumes don't usually stain, but some contain ingredients that can discolour clothing. You won't notice a mark straight away, but it can darken with age. The best preventive measure is to allow perfume to dry completely before you get dressed. Oh, and don't spray it on to disguise those less than fragrant areas of clothing you've already worn a few times... Not that you would ever do such a thing, of course!

General directions If you do notice perfume marks, fresh ones usually come out with normal washing, but rinse the affected area with cold water first to stop the mark being 'set' by hot water in the washing machine. For old stains on washable fabrics, lubricate the stain with a solution of equal parts glycerine and water, leave to soak for up to an hour, then wash as normal. If that doesn't work, try spot-treating the affected area with Stain Devils No. 6, according to the manufacturer's instructions, before rewashing.

Always refer to the Golden Rules of Stain Removal on pages 14–19

Sunscreen

Sunscreen and suntan lotion contain oils to make them moisture-resistant. If they get on clothes, they can be hard to remove and tend to get darker with age. Always let the product dry before getting dressed and wash your hands after applying lotion and before touching any clothing. If you do get a stain, you need to act fast.

General directions For washable fabrics, gently scrape off any solid residue with a blunt knife. Spot-treat the affected area with De.Solv.It (not on silk) according to the manufacturer's instructions. Flush with cool water and rub a little liquid washing detergent into the affected area, then machine-wash on as high a temperature as the fabric allows. For silk, you can try using White Wizard on the stain before washing at 30°C on the delicates cycle.

CAUTION
Always let your sunscreen dry before you get dressed.

WARNING

AROUND THE HOUSE AND OFFICE

Ballpoint pen

We've all had a ballpoint that's leaked and left an angry splodge of ink on our clothing. This ink doesn't usually come out in the wash, and it can spread to other items, so always check clothing carefully before laundering. You might be able to get a small stain out, but it is difficult.

General directions Blot first with dry, white paper towels. For fabrics, place an absorbent pad under the stain. Follow the directions below for specific fabrics.

Carpet and washable fabrics Apply a cotton bud dipped in methylated spirits to the affected area. Don't over-wet. Dab the stain gently, trying not to spread the ink as it dissolves. Blot firmly with paper towels, moving to a clean area of both pad and towel frequently. Repeat until the colour has stopped lifting. Be prepared to make several applications. Flush with cold water, then gently rub White Wizard into any remaining traces, working it in well. Leave for a couple of minutes, then blot with dry paper towels. Press firmly and hold the towel on the mark for several seconds each time. Flush with water. If traces still remain on fabric, try spot-treating the area with Stain Devils No. 1. Follow the manufacturer's instructions, then machine-wash at as high a temperature as the fabric allows.

Last resort If there are still any signs of the ink, try soaking the item in an oxygen-based, colour-safe bleaching product. Follow the manufacturer's instructions and check the garment's care label first.

Leather The Regency at Home Comprehensive Leather Care Kit (see Specialist Product Directory, page 183) makes short work of ballpoint pen (and other stains) on leather furniture and clothing.

Candle wax

The soft light that candles provide may be romantic, but spilt wax is not! Thankfully, the wax is usually quite straightforward to remove, depending on the colour of the candle. Follow our steps below to get the best results.

General directions The wax needs to be as hard as possible before you attempt to remove it – on carpets, cover the affected area with an ice pack or a bag of frozen peas; on fabrics, place the entire item in the freezer for an hour or so. Once the wax is brittle, you will be able to pick off most of it by hand or with a blunt knife. Follow the directions below for specific fabrics.

Carpet To remove the remaining wax deposits, place a sheet of absorbent kitchen paper over the area and iron on a low heat. Don't let the iron touch the carpet pile or it may scorch and melt. Keep moving the paper around for maximum absorption, and continue until all the wax has been soaked up. Remove any resistant colour or stain with a few drops of methylated spirits (test first on an inconspicuous area, as it may discolour the carpet).

Washable fabrics Follow the directions for treating a carpet, but put an absorbent, white paper towel on both sides of the stain. If any colour remains, use methylated spirits on it, then machine-wash the item on as high a temperature as the fabric allows.

Wooden surfaces Chip away at the wax once it is hard, using your fingernail or a plastic spatula. Remove any remaining film with a duster, then polish as normal. If heat-marking has occurred, rub along the wood grain with a metal polish.

Coloured pencil and crayon

Your children's creativity can lead to all sorts of cleaning headaches. Crayon on carpets, walls, clothing – anywhere other than on the paper you provided! If the damage is limited to a small area, you should be able to get rid of it. Crayons usually contain waxy or oily components and pigments. You need to deal with the greasy part first (see Grease-based Stains, page 22).

General directions Remove any solid bits by scraping gently with a blunt knife, and lifting the debris with sticky tape wrapped around your fingers. Follow the directions below for specific fabrics.

Carpet Put several layers of white paper towels on top of the stain and run a warm iron over them. The heat will melt the crayon and it will be absorbed by the towels. Move to a clean patch on the towels frequently. Dab methylated spirits or WD-40 on any remaining traces of colour. Finally, sponge the area with paper towels dipped in a weak solution of detergent, flush with clear water, and blot with clean paper towels to dry.

Washable fabrics Place the stained area on a pad of paper towels and spray it with WD-40. Let it stand for a few minutes, then turn the fabric over and spray the other side. Clean off as much of the crayon as you can with paper towels. Rub a small amount of liquid detergent into the stained area and machine-wash as normal on as high a temperature as the fabric allows. Remove any surviving traces by soaking the item in an oxygen-based, colour-safe bleaching product, according to the manufacturer's instructions. Check the garment's care label and test an inconspicuous area for colourfastness first.

Heat-set stains in tumble-dryer drum If a crayon left in the pocket of an item of clothing has inadvertently found its way into your tumble-dryer and melted, you'll need to clean the dryer's drum to make sure the crayon is not transferred all over your next load of laundry. Spray WD-40 onto a clean cloth and wipe all around the drum to remove the mess. Follow by running a load of dry rags through a drying cycle to ensure the drum is clean. Repeat if necessary.

Painted walls Rub the area with a lightly dampened cloth dipped in White Wizard, toothpaste, or bicarbonate of soda. The slight abrasiveness will shift the crayon. Be very gentle, to avoid damage.

Vinyl wall-coverings, bedheads and radiators Wipe with a damp cloth. If necessary, apply a few drops of WD-40 to dissolve the crayon.

Wallpaper If the stain is small, you may be able to remove it by spraying lightly with WD-40 and wiping it with a cloth dipped in a weak solution of detergent. Be careful not to over-wet the paper and damage it.

Always refer to the Golden Rules of Stain Removal on pages 14–19

tip

ERASABLE CRAYONS
Buy 'erasable' crayons and pencils, such as those made by Crayola. These come with a special eraser that easily removes marks from most surfaces. They also allow kids to make changes to their drawings and correct colouring 'mistakes', so no more starting from scratch!

Correction fluid

Interesting fact: Bette Nesmith Graham, the mother of Michael Nesmith, a member of The Monkees, invented Liquid Paper, a leading brand of correction fluid, in 1951. Not that it helps you to get the stuff out of your clothes. Some brands of correction fluid are water-based and should come out with normal washing. It's those with petroleum in them that can cause problems. Dry-cleaning is recommended, but if you want to try at home, here's what to do.

General directions Allow the product to dry and pick off as much of the deposit as possible, taking care not to snag the fabric. Dab the affected area with paint remover or turpentine to help fade the mark. Flush with water, then treat with a citrus-based, spot-treatment stain remover (such as De.Solv.It) according to the manufacturer's instructions.

Follow the directions below for specific fabrics.

Carpet You may be able to remove the offending area by carefully snipping the tufts off the carpet.

Washable fabrics Machine-wash on as high a temperature as the fabric allows. Don't hold out too much hope, though!

tip

PENCIL VERSUS PEN
Either use a pencil when filling in your crossword or invest in one of those neat, pen-type correction fluid products. They're easier to use, and don't drip, so are less likely to lead to stains.

Felt-tip pen

Another item that children love using all over the house. Anywhere, in fact, they can draw on to express their artistic leanings! Felt-tip is difficult to remove, but if you're persistent and the stain is small, you may be able to get it out.

General directions Blot first with dry paper towels. For fabrics, place an absorbent pad under the stain. Follow the directions below for specific fabrics.

Carpet and washable fabrics Apply a cotton bud dipped in methylated spirits to the affected area. Don't over-wet. Dab gently at the stain, trying not to spread it too much as it's being dissolved. Blot firmly with paper towels, moving to a clean area of both pad and towel frequently. Repeat until no further colour seems to be lifting. Be prepared to make several applications. Flush with cold water, then carefully rub White Wizard into any remaining traces, working it in well. Leave for a couple of minutes, and blot again with dry paper towels. Press the towel firmly against the mark for several seconds each time. Blot with water. On fabric, if traces still remain, try spot-treating the area with Stain Devils No. 1. Follow the manufacturer's instructions, then machine-wash at as high a temperature as the fabric allows.

Last resort If there are still any signs of the ink, try soaking the item in an oxygen-based, colour-safe bleaching product. Follow the manufacturer's instructions and check the garment's care label first.

Glue

This is a sticky one! There are lots of different types of glue, so the treatment will depend on which type has caused the stain. If possible, follow the removal procedures given on the glue's packaging or contact the manufacturer for specific advice. Otherwise, try the methods below.

General directions Quickly and gently scrape off the glue with a blunt knife and paper towels.

All-purpose household adhesive Dab the affected area with acetone (nail polish remover) until the glue has dissolved. Launder (where possible).

Contact adhesive These harden on contact, so you must act fast. Treat as for all-purpose adhesives.

Epoxy resin This consists of a glue and a hardener. Once epoxy resin has hardened, it is almost impossible to remove. Use acetone (nail polish remover) or methylated spirits to remove it before it sets.

Paper adhesive and latex glue Pick off the glue residue first. For carpets, dab the stain with a liquid detergent solution – do not over-wet. Rinse and blot dry. For fabrics, wash as normal.

Superglue For carpets, sponge the area with warm, soapy water to dissolve the glue – you may have to do this several times. Do not over-wet. Blot afterwards to dry. If this doesn't work, try dabbing the area with nail polish remover, but test a hidden area of the carpet for colourfastness first. For washable fabrics, dab with nail polish remover to dissolve the glue (having tested for colourfastness), then machine-wash as normal.

Heat rings and watermarks on wooden furniture

There's always someone who manages to miss the coaster and put their steaming-hot cup of coffee or their cold drink down directly on your polished mahogany table, leaving an ugly heat ring or watermark underneath. Don't get mad – just don't invite them back! Here's what to do.

Solution If the surface has roughened, try smoothing it by rubbing it with very fine steel wool dipped in liquid wax polish, working in the direction of the grain. On veneered finishes, use this method with extreme care. If the surface is not rough, put a dab of a cream metal polish on a cloth and rub the wood briskly in the direction of the grain. Work on small sections at a time, wiping away the cream at intervals to check progress. Finish by polishing the table lightly with wax polish.

If nothing works Try disguising the mark by rubbing a little shoe polish of an appropriate colour into the mark, then buff with furniture polish.

Blisters in veneer These can sometimes be flattened by covering them with a cotton tea towel and ironing them. Leave for two days to see if there is an improvement.

Always refer to the Golden Rules of Stain Removal on pages 14–19

Ink

Trying to explain how to remove ink is difficult because there are so many different types that it's impossible to provide one foolproof method. Your first port of call should be the manufacturer, who may be able to provide you with instructions specifically designed for the product. If so, follow these. Otherwise, the product many ink manufacturers seem to recommend is Amodex Ink and Stain Remover. If you can get hold of this (see the Specialist Product Directory, page 183), wait until you have it before trying to remove the stain – it's claimed to work as well on dry stains, and other methods used in the interim may reduce its effectiveness. Always follow the manufacturer's instructions. If you can't wait, the following tried-and-tested methods are the most likely to succeed. Unfortunately, 'permanent ink' usually means just that! (See also Felt-tip pen, page 149.)

General directions Blot first with dry paper towels. For fabrics, place an absorbent pad under the stain.

Carpet and washable fabrics Apply a cotton bud, dipped in methylated spirits, to the affected area. Don't over-wet. Dab the stain gently, trying not to spread it as it is being dissolved. Blot firmly with paper towels, moving to a clean area of both pad and towel frequently. Repeat until no further colour seems to be lifting. Be prepared to make several applications. Flush with cold water, then rub White Wizard into any remaining traces, working it in well. Leave for a couple of minutes, and blot again with dry paper towels. Press the towel firmly against the mark for several seconds each time. Flush with water. On fabric, if traces still remain, try spot-treating the area with Stain Devils No. 1, following the manufacturer's instructions, then machine-wash at as high a temperature as the fabric allows.

Household surfaces Rub away as much of the mark as you can with a sponge dipped in soapy water. If the stain persists, use a white paper towel dampened with methylated spirits, working from the outside inwards.

On leather The Regency at Home Comprehensive Leather Care Kit (see Specialist Product Directory, page 183) can be used to remove ink and all sorts of other stains on leather furniture and clothing.

Last resort If there are still any signs of the ink, try soaking the item in an oxygen-based, colour-safe bleaching solution. Follow the manufacturer's instructions and check the garment's care label first.

Special instructions for red ink If the above methods don't work, try spot-treating the affected area with Wine Away (see Specialist Product Directory).

tip

INKY FINGERS
Got inky fingers after a burst of artistic creativity? Try squeezing shampoo onto the affected area and lathering it up with a little water. Use a pumice stone to gently abrade the stained parts of your hands. Keep going until all the ink is removed, then rinse well under cool running water.

Limescale

If you live in a hard water area, dealing with limescale can feel like a never-ending battle. Those ugly, scaly deposits build up quickly on kitchen and bathroom fittings, pipes and appliances. You can use proprietary descalers, but ordinary white vinegar will often do the job just as well and is also a more environmentally friendly option.

Kettles Fill the kettle with a solution consisting of half water and half vinegar, and leave it overnight. In the morning, the limescale will come off easily. Rinse thoroughly to remove any vinegary odours.

Showerheads Try soaking the showerhead overnight in a solution of half water and half white vinegar. Rinse with plain water after soaking and use a needle to poke any remaining scale out of the jet holes.

Taps and bathroom fittings Make up a spray bottle of half vinegar and half water, and use it regularly on tiles, basins, baths and taps to keep limescale at bay. Always rinse thoroughly with plain water afterwards. Don't use it on plated taps, particularly gold – the acid in vinegar can damage their finish.

Toilets On ceramic toilets, try removing very heavy limescale deposits by rubbing gently with a pumice stone.

tip

MORE INFORMATION
Find more tips on removing limescale in Part 2: Preventive Measures, page 36.

Marble stains

The chances are you paid an arm and a leg for that gleaming kitchen worktop, so keep it clean and look after it. Always wipe up spills immediately, rinse off cleaning products with clean water and buff dry. Stones such as marble aren't as tough as you think. They are quite  porous and can easily be damaged by highly coloured and acidic foods. If you do get a stain, it will be hard to remove and you may need to call in a specialist. Here's what you can try at home first.

Oily stains Make a thickish paste from bicarbonate of soda and water and apply it to the affected area, overlapping the edges of the mark slightly. Cover with clingfilm and seal the edges with masking tape. Leave to dry thoroughly – it is the drying action that draws the stain from the stone. This will usually take from twenty-four to forty-eight hours. Once dry, remove the paste, rinse the area with water and dry with a soft cloth. If the stain is still there, repeat the process. It may take up to five applications.

Coloured stains Cover stains made by foods such as beetroot with a few drops of hydrogen peroxide (available from most pharmacies). Cover with clingfilm as above and leave overnight, then rinse with clean water and buff dry. Repeat if necessary.

Restore shine If either method dulls the surface of the stone, you can restore the shine with a proprietary marble polish.

Acid stains Marks caused by acidic foods such as lemon juice, vinegar, or cola are harder to deal with. You can try using a specialized marble cleaner, but unfortunately it's likely that the area will need to be professionally repolished.

Mould and mildew

 It's not a pretty sight when you discover furry black spores on clothes and in other areas of your home. Mould and mildew thrive in damp, humid conditions where there is inadequate ventilation. Stop them sprouting in the first place by keeping the house dry and well aired. If certain parts suffer from high levels of condensation, consider buying a de-humidifier. If moulds and mildew do appear, here's how to tackle them.

Carpet Brush or vacuum away spores and spray with a proprietary fungicide suitable for soft furnishings. Dab remaining marks with a mild disinfectant until they have been removed, then sponge with cold water to rinse.

Washable fabrics Normal washing should remove light stains when they are fresh. Treat stubborn stains on white fabric (except nylon and items with a 'do not bleach' symbol) by soaking in a solution of chlorine bleach (20ml bleach to 5 litres water). Treat coloureds and non-bleachable whites with a stain remover such as Stain Devils No. 7, following the manufacturer's instructions.

More information Find more information on dealing with mould on other surfaces in the section on bathrooms in Part 2: Preventive Measures, page 36.

> **To avoid mould and mildew, keep the house dry and well aired**

Paint

So you've just had a new carpet fitted and have decided that now is a good time to redecorate – after all, the new flooring is making everything else around the house look drab. However, little splashes of paint have found their way on to not only the carpet, but  also your clothes and just about everything else. Some paints are more amenable to removal than others. Just keep your fingers crossed that yours is one of the easy ones.

General directions If possible, refer to the paint manufacturer's instructions for removing stains and follow these. If there are no instructions and the paint is still wet, blot with paper towels to remove as much of it as possible.

Acrylic paint Wash out with detergent and water. If the stain has dried, place an absorbent pad under it, if possible, and dab with paper towels moistened with methylated spirits. Flush with cold water, then wash at as high a temperature as the fabric allows.

Oil-based paint Almost impossible to remove, but you can try holding an absorbent pad under the stain and dabbing it with white spirit. Afterwards, sponge with water (if on carpet) or wash at as high a temperature as the fabric allows. If the stain remains, consult a dry-cleaner.

Water-based paint Rinse out or flush fresh marks with cold water, then launder. Dried marks are difficult to remove, but treating with a proprietary paint remover may fade them.

Shoe polish

Your husband kindly offered to polish your shoes while he was doing his own. Unfortunately, he cleaned them while sitting in front of the TV. Now the carpet is covered with greasy black marks. Don't worry: you should be able to get them out without too much difficulty.

General directions Carefully scrape up any solid bits with a blunt knife. Follow the directions below for specific fabrics.

Carpet Squirt a few drops of WD-40 on the affected area, wait thirty seconds, then blot with white paper towels, moving to clean areas of the towel frequently. Work from the outside inwards, and use a delicate dabbing motion. You must be gentle to avoid pushing the stain deeper in or spreading it. Repeat as necessary until no more of the stain is lifted. Remove remaining traces of colour with White Wizard. Apply and leave for a minute or so, then blot the stain with lightly dampened, white paper towels or a clean, white, lint-free cloth. Finish by dabbing

the area with clean water to rinse it, then blot it dry. You may have to make several applications.

Washable fabrics A small stain on cotton will often come out simply by rubbing in a little liquid detergent and washing as normal. For larger stains, pre-treat with Stain Devils No. 5 according to the manufacturer's instructions, then wash at 40°C with biological detergent. Shoe polish is difficult to remove from silk, but try the WD-40 method as described for carpet, followed by Stain Devils No. 3 to remove any greasy mark left by the WD-40. Machine-wash at 30°C on the delicates cycle. For wool, spot-treat with Stain Devils No. 5 and wash at 30°C on the delicates cycle.

Sticky tape and labels

Why haven't stores realized how irritating those sticky price labels are to customers, when it comes to trying to remove them from precious purchases at home? You've ruined your nails picking off as much as you can, worked up a sweat scrubbing at it, and even tried soaking it with hot water, but there's still a dirty, sticky residue that refuses to budge.

The solution Easy. Just spray the affected area with WD-40 or Sticky Stuff Remover and leave it for thirty seconds or so, then give it a wipe and the sticky stuff will come right off. Repeat if necessary. If the tape or sticker has been there for a long time, you might also need to make use of a plastic scraper to banish it once and for all.

If the mark is on an item that is used for food or drink, such as glasses, pans etc, and you are uncomfortable using solvents on something you will be eating from, then try this more natural method instead. Make a paste of two parts bicarbonate of soda and one part water and apply it to the affected area. The abrasive action of the bicarbonate of soda is very effective for removing some types of sticky stuff.

CAUTION
When using any cleaning agents, wear rubber gloves if you have sensitive skin. Always wear them when handling corrosive chemicals.

WARNING

THE
GREAT
OUTDOORS

Bicycle and car grease

Cycling is a great way to get around and good exercise to boot. However, you have to keep a bike well oiled and this can lead to oily messes. Bicycle grease forms a stain similar to that of shoe polish and contains both oils and pigment.

General directions Carefully scrape up any solid bits with a blunt knife. Follow the directions below for specific fabrics.

Carpet Squirt a few drops of WD-40 on the affected area, wait about thirty seconds, then blot with paper towels, moving to clean areas of the towel frequently. Work from the outside inwards, and use a delicate dabbing motion. You must be gentle, so that you do not push the stain deeper into the carpet or spread it. Repeat as necessary until no more of the stain is lifted. Remove remaining traces of colour with White Wizard. Apply the product to the mark and leave it for a minute or so, then blot with lightly dampened paper towels or a clean white cloth. Finish by dabbing the area with clean water to rinse it, then blot dry. Be prepared to make several applications before the stain is completely removed.

Washable fabrics If the stain is very small and faint, it may come out simply by rubbing in a little liquid detergent, then washing as normal. For larger, darker stains, try using the WD-40 method as described for carpet, followed by spot-treatment with Stain Devils No. 3 to remove the greasy mark that may be left by the WD-40. Then machine-wash on as hot a temperature as the fabric will allow.

Grass

Picnics in the park are one of the greatest pleasures of summer, but the resulting grass stains can be troublesome. Grass stains are mainly a mixture of chlorophyll and proteins, and it's the pigment in the chlorophyll that is hard to shift, particularly from delicate fabrics such as silk.

Washable fabrics For cotton, rub White Wizard into the affected area and blot with white paper towels to remove as much colour as you can. Reapply the product, then machine-wash at 40°C with biological detergent. You must act quickly to get a grass stain out of silk. Again, use White Wizard, following the directions for cotton, then machine-wash at 30°C on the delicates cycle. For wool, spot-treat the affected area with Stain Devils No. 5, according to the manufacturer's instructions. Follow by machine-washing the item at 30°C on the delicates cycle. You can also use White Wizard for grass stains on wool.

tip

STAINS ON SHOES
For grass stains on white leather trainers or tennis shoes, try spraying the stained area with a few drops of WD-40 and wiping with a clean cloth.

Mud

Mud can be as variable as the earth itself, and contains a mixture of soiling agents: clay, loam, proteins and pigments, even grease. Enzyme-based stain removers tend to work well on the organic components in stubborn mud stains, but remember that you can't use them on silk and wool. Act fast, particularly with delicate fabrics, or you may have a permanent souvenir.

General directions Allow the mud to dry, then remove as much as possible by brushing or vacuuming the affected area. Follow the directions below for specific fabrics.

Carpet Apply White Wizard and allow it to work for a few minutes. Blot with lightly dampened paper towels. Repeat as necessary until the stain has been removed. Rinse with clear water and blot dry.

Washable fabrics Often, the stain will come out of cotton simply by machine-washing it at 40°C with a biological detergent. For more stubborn stains, try a biological pre-soaking product. Follow the manufacturer's instructions, then wash the item as normal. For silk and wool, try rubbing a little washing-up liquid into the affected area before washing as normal. If this doesn't work, spot-treat with Stain Devils No. 5, according to the manufacturer's instructions, then wash as normal.

Last resort Soak the item in an oxygen-based, colour-safe bleaching product. Follow the instructions given by the manufacturer and check the garment's care label first.

Pollen

Having flowers around the house is uplifting, but pollen can be dangerous. Lilies are probably the worst offender. They smell exquisite, but the mess made by their pollen is less appealing. You can get rid of it – but if it has landed on textiles, it is essential to avoid pushing the powdery pollen deeper into the fibre.

General directions Don't rub or wet the stain. Instead, gently pat the affected area with sticky tape wrapped around your fingers, or vacuum up the pollen using the crevice nozzle. Follow the directions below for specific fabrics.

Carpet Cover any remaining traces with White Wizard and blot with white paper towels. Rinse by dabbing with clean towels dampened with water, then blot dry.

Washable fabrics For cotton and wool, all you need to do after the sticky tape treatment is to machine-wash the item at as high a temperature as the fabric allows, using the appropriate programme. For silk, after removing the dry debris with sticky tape, spot-treat any remaining traces with Stain Devils No. 1, according to the manufacturer's instructions. Follow by machine-washing at 30°C on the delicates cycle.

tip

DELICATE REMOVAL
You can use the sticky tape method to remove other powdery, delicate things such as spider webs and crumbs. It's also good for lifting pet hairs from fabrics.

Rust and iron mould

 Rust is the common name for iron oxide, a substance that occurs when iron corrodes in the presence of oxygen and water. It often occurs when a lot of iron is present in the water supply. The resulting stain is a characteristic reddish-brown colour and can be difficult to remove. Try the methods below.

General directions The traditional way to deal with rust stains is to apply salt and lemon juice to the stain and leave it in the sun. Keep the stained area moistened with lemon juice until the mark disappears, then allow it to dry and brush away the salt. Or you can try the remedies below.

Carpet Use a solution of warm water and biological detergent (ten parts water to one part detergent), testing first on a hidden area. If the stain does not come out, try a stronger solution, but avoid over-wetting the carpet. Alternatively, try applying a mixture of lemon juice and salt to the stained area. This will help to fade it. Rinse or vacuum away the salt afterwards.

Washable fabrics Rust stains on clothes that have been through the washing machine are likely to be iron mould – a mould that develops if a rusty mark is left

> **CAUTION**
> Never try to remove a rust stain with chlorine bleach – it will set the stain permanently.
>
> **WARNING**

untreated. If your washing machine is old, it may be responsible – check for rust marks before and after clothes go in the wash. Wash clothes as normal to remove light marks. Treat heavily marked areas with a proprietary rust and iron mould remover, such as Stain Devils No. 7. Follow the manufacturer's instructions and finish by washing at as high a temperature as the fabric allows. Iron mould is easily transferred from one garment to another, so be vigilant and treat affected clothes as soon as you spot them.

Concrete patios and driveways
These marks appear when ferrous (iron-containing) materials come into contact with the concrete and leave traces that, when combined with oxygen and water, cause rust to form. A common culprit is garden fertilizer, which often contains iron. The best way to remove them is with a phosphoric acid-based specialist cleaner. These are available in most hardware stores. Phosphoric acid is toxic and can burn the skin and eyes, so be careful to follow the manufacturer's instructions to the letter, and always wear gloves and safety goggles. You should also avoid using stiff wire brushes because these can leave metal traces in the concrete that later cause rust to appear. Use a bristle brush instead.

Enamelled baths made of cast iron or steel Rust stains can be reduced by rubbing with a paste of bicarbonate of soda and water – leave it on for one hour, then rinse off. Lemon juice and salt also work well. Rinse or vacuum away the salt afterwards.

Salt marks and watermarks on textiles

The rains and snows of winter weather are often the cause of these marks. Stains caused by salt and water can be hard to shift, so try to stop them appearing by waterproofing outdoor clothing regularly.

Fabrics Remove watermarks from viscose by wetting the whole garment to give a uniform finish. This is also worth trying on non-washable silk if the dry-cleaner can't help remove a mark: you've nothing to lose.

Suede or leather garments Let the item dry naturally at normal room temperature in a well-ventilated room. Brush out marks on suede and even out the colour with a suede brush. On leather, use a proprietary leather-cleaning product.

Suede or leather shoes Moisten the stain and rub with a soft cloth, or try a proprietary cleaner. After treatment, spray shoes with a water-repellent.

Always refer to the Golden Rules of Stain Removal on pages 14–19

Soot

Barbecues, fires and smoke can all produce soot stains. Here are some remedies for removing them, but if you don't manage to fix the problem yourself, some dry-cleaners offer special ozone treatments to remove smoke and soot damage.

General directions Soot particles can be very fine and you may cause further damage by trying to brush them away. Instead, use the nozzle attachment of the vacuum cleaner to pick up the residue. Sprinkle talcum powder over the area to absorb the stain – rub in lightly, then vacuum away the deposit. Follow the directions below for specific fabrics.

Carpet If stains remain, try spot-treating with a proprietary carpet stain remover such as Bissell OxyKIC. You may need to have the whole carpet professionally shampooed.

Washable fabrics After vacuuming up debris, wash as normal at as high a temperature as the fabric allows. Keep the load small, so that clothing has plenty of room to move about, and don't use fabric conditioner until all odours have been removed, otherwise it will mask them. If the stain remains, carry on laundering the item until it disappears – you may have to rewash several times. Try not to let the item dry out between washes.

Stubborn stains Soak garments overnight in a suitable pre-soak, or for thirty minutes in an oxygen-based, colour-safe bleaching solution, following the manufacturer's instructions. Check the garments' care labels first.

Tar

This sticky, icky black stuff gets traipsed into your house after nearby roads have been resurfaced. Watch out for it after a trip to the beach, too – for some reason, it often seems to be found in sand!

General directions Scrape carefully with a blunt knife to remove surface deposits. Follow the directions below for specific fabrics.

Carpet Tar that has hardened may need softening first with a solution made up of equal parts of water and glycerine. Leave for up to an hour, then rinse with clean water and blot well. Then use a proprietary carpet cleaner, such as Bissell OxyKIC, following the manufacturer's instructions.

Washable fabrics Hold an absorbent pad (such as a wad of paper towels) over the stain and dab it from underneath with paper towels moistened with eucalyptus oil (available from pharmacies).

WD-40 also works well. Move to a clean area of the pad and towels frequently. Repeat until no more of the stain transfers to the towels. Rub liquid detergent into the remnants of the stain, and machine-wash on as high a temperature as the fabric allows.

Stubborn traces Soak the item in an oxygen-based, colour-safe bleaching product. Check the garment's care label first and always follow the manufacturer's instructions.

On surfaces Spray a little WD-40 on the affected area and leave for thirty seconds. Wipe away carefully with a clean, damp cloth.

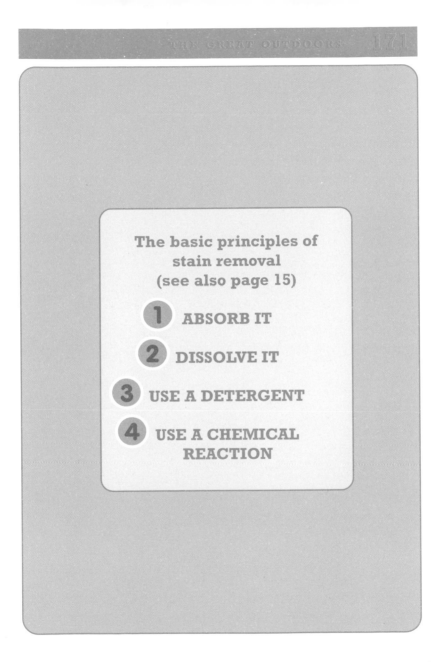

The basic principles of
stain removal
(see also page 15)

1 ABSORB IT

2 DISSOLVE IT

3 USE A DETERGENT

4 USE A CHEMICAL
REACTION

LIFE'S LITTLE ACCIDENTS

Bird droppings

We all love birds, don't we? That beautiful singing, the way they dart and swoop... but oh, what's that? Yes, an oozing dollop of guano has appeared from above to land, where else, but on the shoulder of your best suit! And suddenly, birds just don't seem so appealing. Don't worry; this is one humiliation that's easy to deal with.

General directions Gently scrape off as much dirt as possible with a blunt knife or paper towels. Follow the directions below for specific fabrics.

Washable fabrics The marks usually come out in a normal machine-wash. If they do not, try soaking the affected item in an oxygen-based, colour-safe bleaching product. Check the garment's care label first and follow the bleach manufacturer's instructions.

Canvas and awnings Allow to dry thoroughly, then remove the dirt with a stiff brush. If marks remain, dip the brush in a solution of biological washing detergent and rub the affected area. Hose down and rinse well.

> ⚠️ **WARNING**
>
> **PROTECT YOUR CAR**
> Always remove bird droppings from your car the instant that they appear. If they are left for more than a day or so, the acid in the droppings will eat into the top coat of paint and cause permanent damage. Be prepared: keep a bottle of spray cleaner and paper towels in the glove compartment.

Blood

One of the most common stains, particularly for women. Don't panic, because blood is easy to remove if you treat it while it is still fresh. The most important thing to remember is that it is a protein-based stain and therefore must be treated at a low wash temperature. This stops the protein coagulating and setting the stain into the fabric.

General directions Gently blot up as much of the stain as possible with white paper towels or a clean, white, lint-free cloth. Dab, rather than rub, at the stain. Follow the directions below for specific fabrics.

Carpet Cover the stain with Wine Away and, working from the outside inwards, use white paper towels or a clean, white, lint-free cloth to absorb the stain. Make repeated small applications rather than soaking the area. Continue until the stain has gone. If traces remain, try covering the affected area with a paste of cornflour or un-pigmented meat tenderizer and water. Leave to dry, sponge off with cold water and repeat.

Washable fabrics Enzyme-based pre-soaking agents and biological detergents can be used, but are often unsuitable for use on silk and wool, so check the care label. For fresh blood, after blotting, rinse the stain under cold water. If the stain has dried, steep first in an enzyme-based, pre-soaking agent, or a washing soda crystal solution (for silk and cotton), then follow the instructions given for each fabric. For cotton, machine-wash at 40°C with biological detergent. For silk, machine-wash at 30°C on the delicates cycle. For wool, spray lightly with Wine Away until the stain turns blue. Blot again, and repeat this process until the stain has gone. Follow with a 30°C machine-wash on a delicates cycle.

Excrement

Nappies are the most common offender, but you might also have a problem with an aged pet who is not quite as good at asking to go outside as he used to be. Excrement is a protein-based stain and not usually difficult to remove, providing you use a low wash temperature. As always, the main thing is to act fast. Wear rubber gloves to remove the poop and dispose of it down the toilet.

Carpet Blot with paper towels dipped in a solution of bicarbonate of soda and water, to which you have added a few drops of disinfectant. Blot dry. If necessary, clean and deodorize the area with a proprietary pet stain remover (available from pet supply stores). Spray with a solution of one part white vinegar to five parts water, to deter your pet from returning to do his business on the same spot.

Washable fabrics Scrape away the deposit and blot dry. If it is not possible to remove the item for cleaning, isolate the stain by tying string tightly around the fabric and gathering it up. Rinse under cold running water. Sanitize by blotting with disinfectant solution or treat with a proprietary pet stain remover. Otherwise, machine-wash the item as normal.

Stained nappies and underwear Scrape away any deposits. Rinse promptly in cold water to minimize staining. Soak in a solution of bicarbonate of soda and water to help remove and deodorize stains. If possible, machine-wash with biological detergent – the enzymes are effective on the protein in excrement. To sanitize the garment, wash at a temperature of 60°C or above, but such a high temperature may mean you will be left with the stain.

Semen

The joy of sex is not without a downside. Someone always gets the damp patch, and will probably have to clear up afterwards. Don't be caught out like **Bill Clinton**! Deal with a semen stain promptly and it won't come back to haunt you (see Protein-based stains, page 24).

Carpet Oh naughty you. Next time, try to contain your passion until you get to the bedroom! Semen stains in the carpet should come out easily by sponging the affected area with a cool water and detergent solution. Follow by rinsing, then blotting with dry paper towels to remove as much moisture as possible. Leave to dry naturally. If any powdery, dry matter remains, use a soft brush to remove it.

Washable fabrics Fresh stains are usually removed easily by rinsing with cold water. It's important to use cold water because higher temperatures can coagulate the protein in semen and set it into the fabric fibres, causing a permanent stain. If the stains are old or crusted and on any fabric other than silk or wool, remove any dry matter first with a soft brush, then steep in an enzyme-based pre-soaking agent before laundering as normal.

Silk and wool For old stains on silk and wool, make up a pre-soaking solution of water containing a detergent for delicates and leave to soak before washing as normal.

> **Always refer to the Golden Rules of Stain Removal on pages 14–19**

Sweat

Stumped by how to remove those nasty, smelly perspiration stains from the underarms of your husband's work shirts? This is one situation where prevention really is better than cure, because the stains really are hard to shift. You can stop them appearing by rinsing affected areas with cold water, or by dabbing them with a little white vinegar, before each wash. Clean garments as soon as possible after wearing. For older, yellowed stains, try the methods below, but be prepared for limited success.

Non-washable fabrics For light soiling, dab with a solution of white vinegar (15ml vinegar to 250ml warm water) to help to clean and deodorize the area; however this may also cause watermarks. Dry-cleaning is a better option.

Washable fabrics For cotton, immerse in an enzyme-based pre-soaking agent. Scrub affected areas with a nailbrush, and then machine-wash with a biological detergent, adding an in-wash stain remover to the load. For stubborn stains, rub with a solution made up of half glycerine and half warm water, and leave for an hour before washing

as previously described. Or, try using a nailbrush to work White Wizard into the affected areas before you put the garment into the machine. Unfortunately, nothing works very well on silk and wool, but with light staining, you may have some success with the glycerine or White Wizard methods described for cotton.

Removing odours If odours remain even after washing, try soaking the offending garment for thirty minutes in a sink filled with cool water containing 5 or 6 tbsp of bicarbonate of soda. Wash again and allow to dry naturally.

Other things to try If the previous suggestions don't work, you can try these more unusual tips too.

Aspirin Use this one on white cotton shirts. Take two soluble, white, uncoated aspirin and dissolve them in half a mugful of water. Apply to the stained area and leave to soak for a couple of hours. Rub a little liquid detergent into the stain, then wash as normal.

Meat tenderizer Not as mad as you might think when you consider that perspiration is a protein-based stain and meat tenderizer works by breaking down proteins! Dampen the stained area with water and apply half a teaspoon of

> Always refer to the Golden Rules of Stain Removal on pages 14–19

tenderizer powder. Allow to stand for thirty minutes, then wash as normal.

Lemon juice Squeeze the juice from a lemon and add an equal amount of water to it. Apply to the stained area and scrub in well with a nailbrush. Place in a sunny area and allow to dry – the lemon juice and sunlight are both good bleaching agents and will help fade the stain. Follow by washing as normal.

tip

STAY FRESH
Shower or bath daily, and use sweat guards or pads in the underarms of your clothes to prevent them from coming into contact with perspiration. These are usually available in department stores such as John Lewis, or good pharmacies.

Urine

You love your kitty, but wish he wasn't so determined to stake out his territory in the house by spraying everywhere. While we're on the subject, why is it that cats always seem to find mattresses, sofas and other soft furnishings the most appealing receptacles for their offerings? Why can't they just use the kitty-tray lavatory you've so thoughtfully provided? It's a tough one, but with a bit of effort, you should be able to remove the stain, and the smell.

Carpet Flush the affected area with cold water and blot until nearly dry. Sponge with a proprietary carpet cleaner, such as Bissell OxyKIC. Rinse well with cold water containing a few drops of disinfectant. Blot to dry.

Mattresses Hold the mattress on its side and sponge with a cold solution of washing-up liquid or upholstery shampoo. Wipe with cold water containing a few drops of disinfectant.

Non-washable fabrics Remove fresh stains by sponging with a vinegar solution (15ml vinegar to 500ml water). Dried stains should be cleaned professionally.

⚠️
WARNING

CAT URINE
Never use ammonia to clean stains from cat urine – there is ammonia in cat urine, so cats will identify with the smell and go again!

Washable fabrics Rinse the stained area with cold water, then soak overnight in a solution of biological detergent. Machine-wash as normal.

If the pong persists The smell can be particularly difficult to get rid of. This is because the uric acid crystals and salts in cat urine are insoluble and bond tightly with any surface they land on, making them very resistant to regular household cleaning agents. If any type of moisture gets on the crystals, they are activated and release that 'tom cat' aroma – this also explains why the smell becomes particularly strong in humid weather conditions. The only way to completely get rid of the smell is with an enzyme-based cleaner designed specifically for pet urine. These usually also come with a special ultraviolet light torch that can show you exactly how far your pet has sprayed. There are lots of brands available – ask a vet or pet supply store which one they recommend.

Always refer to the Golden Rules of Stain Removal on pages 14–19

LEAKY TODDLER TIP
If you have a 'leaky' toddler who's prone to night-time mishaps, consider investing in waterproof mattress covers that prevent urine from seeping through to the mattress below. That way, you'll just have the sheets to deal with!

tip

Vomit

Crisp white linen shirt been blessed with one of your toddler's finest technicolour yawns? The joys of small children! We love them dearly, but sometimes they really do try us. Vomit can be a problem: it's a complex stain containing acids, proteins, colours and other components (not to mention the awful smell), and you need to act quickly to ensure that it doesn't leave a lasting reminder.

Carpet Scoop up as much as possible and clean with a solution of bicarbonate of soda. Blot well. Spot-treat with a proprietary carpet cleaner such as Bissell OxyKIC. Follow the manufacturer's instructions and make repeat applications until the stain has cleared. Rinse with warm water containing a few drops of disinfectant. Blot well. If the odour persists, try sprinkling the area with bicarbonate of soda. Leave for a few hours, then vacuum up.

Washable fabrics Remove the deposit and rinse well, from the back of the stain, with cold water. Machine-wash as normal, using biological detergent if possible.

Stubborn stains For cottons, try soaking in an enzyme-based pre-soaking agent. For silk and wool, soak in a solution of a suitable detergent for delicates. Always follow the manufacturer's instructions and check the garment's care label first.

> **Act quickly to avoid a lasting reminder**

4

Specialist product directory

Amodex Ink and Stain Remover

Available from The Battersea Pen Home
www.penhome.co.uk
tel: 01992 578 885
Specialist ink stain remover.

Bar Keepers Friend

www.homecareproducts.co.uk
tel: 01473 832 020
Stain remover for household surfaces, particularly stainless steel.

Bissell OxyKIC Carpet Spot and Stain Remover

Bissell
www.bissell.com
tel: 0870 2250109
Specialist carpet cleaner.

Dasco

www.dunkelman.com
tel: 01536 760760
Fabric cleaners for leather and suede.

De.Solv.It

Available from Mykal Industries
www.desolvit.com
tel: 01933 402 822
Natural citrus stain remover.

Dylon Stain Solve

Dylon
www.dylon.co.uk
tel: 020 8663 4801
Good all-purpose stain remover.

Hob Brite

www.homecareproducts.co.uk
tel: 01473 832 020
Cleaner for ceramic and halogen hobs.

Regency at Home Comprehensive Leather Care Kit

Available from Homeserve. Mail order only.
tel: 0870 320 0244
Complete leather care.

Stain Devils Nos 1–8 and Stain Removing Wipes

Available from Acdoco Ltd
www.staindevils.co.uk
tel: 01204 600 500
Stain-specific spot removers.

Sticky Stuff Remover

Available from Lakeland Limited
www.lakelandlimited.co.uk
tel: 015394 88100
For removing chewing gum, sticky tape and labels.

WD-40

Available from www.WD40.co.uk
tel: 01908 555 400
Works well on greasy stains, and dissolves chewing gum and sticky label residue.

White Wizard

Available from Lakeland Limited
www.lakelandlimited.com
tel: 015394 88100
Excellent all-purpose stain remover.

Wine Away

Available from Lakeland Limited
www.lakelandlimited.com
tel: 015394 88100
Removes red wine and other stains.

SERVICE PROVIDERS

Association of Master Upholsterers

www.upholsterers.co.uk
tel: 01633 215 454
Advice and directory of craftspeople for repairs and restorations of upholstered furniture.

British Antique Restorers' Association

www.bafra.org.uk
tel: 01305 854 822
Directory of specialist craftspeople for repairs and restoration of all kinds of antiques.

Jeeves of Belgravia

www.jeevesofbelgravia.co.uk
tel: 020 8809 3232
Vacuum packing service for wedding dresses and other special garments.

Leather Master
www.leathermasteruk.com
tel: 0115 973 7280
*Supplier of leather cleaning products
and repair service.*

Renubath Services Ltd
www.renubath.co.uk
tel: 0800 138 2202
Bath re-enamelling service.

Royal School of Needlework
www.royal-needlework.co.uk
tel: 020 8943 1432
*Repair and restoration of antique
textiles.*

Servicemaster
www.servicemaster.co.uk
tel: 0116 275 9000
*Network of franchised carpet and
upholstery cleaning firms.*

Textiles Services Association
www.tsa-uk.org
tel: 020 8863 8658
*Professional body for dry-cleaners in
the UK. Can provide a list of specialist
dry-cleaning services in your area.*

PROFESSIONAL BODY

Home Laundering Consultative Council
www.care-labelling.co.uk,
*HLCC is concerned with the after-care
(ie laundering and dry cleaning) of
clothes and textiles and in particular
care labelling.*

5

Index

Index

Page numbers in **bold** indicate a main entry for a particular stain or stain removal treatment.

The information in this book is based on the work of the Good Housekeeping Institute's Consumer Team, past and present, including: Karen Baker, Emma Burton, Helen Harrison, Jessica Hunt, Clare Livingstone, Jacquelyn Redpath, Patricia Schofield and Deirdre Taylor.

Helen Harrison is a trained home economist and was a Consumer Researcher in the GHI. She is now freelance and is a regular contributor to *Good Housekeeping* – on stains, pests and green cleaning methods.

Acknowledgements

With thanks to the HLCC (Home Laundering Consultative Council) for the information on laundry symbols on pages 55–57.